Animals & Flowers

Adult Coloring Book

Golden Age Press

VISIT US ONLINE:

WWW.GOLDENAGEPRESS.COM

© 2023 Barbara House
Published by Golden Age Press
goldenagepress.com All Rights Reserved.

No part of this publication may be reproduced, stored in a retrieval system or transmitted in any form or by any means, electronic, mechanical, photocopying, recording, scanning or otherwise, except as permitted under Section 107 or 108 of the 1976 United States Copyright Act, without the prior written permission of the Publisher.

Limit of Liability / Disclaimer of Warranty: The Publisher and the author make no representations or warranties with respect to the accuracy or completeness of the contents of this work and specifically disclaim all warranties, including without limitation warranties of fitness for a particular purpose. No warranty may be created or extended by sales or promotional marketing materials.

Every effort has been made by the author and publisher to ensure that the information contained in this book was correct as of press time. The author and publisher hereby disclaim and do not assume liability for any injury, loss, damage, or disruption caused by errors or omissions, regardless of whether any errors or omissions resulting from negligence, accident, or any other cause. Readers are encouraged to verify any information contained in this book prior to taking any action on the information.

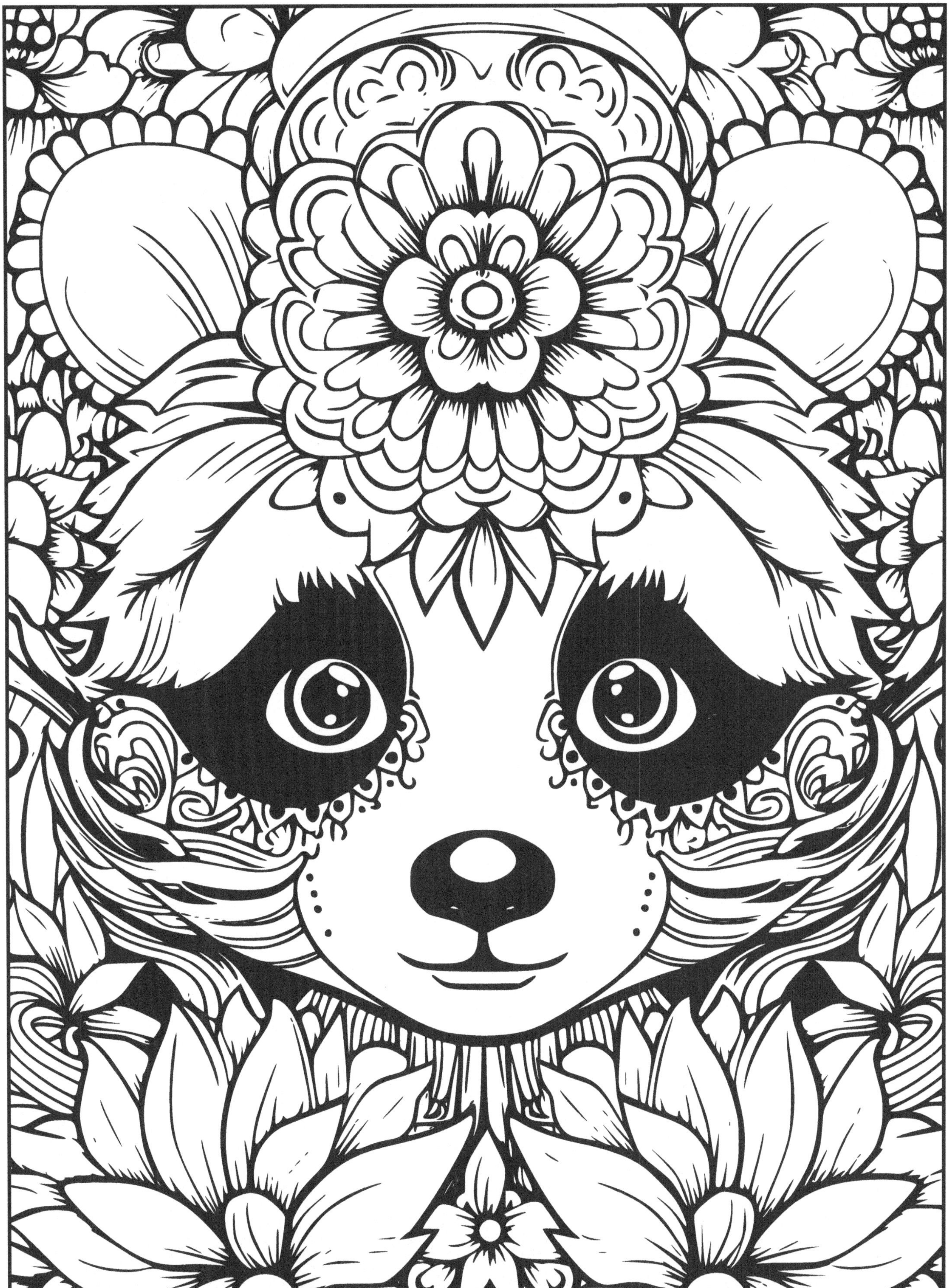

(This page intentionally left blank)

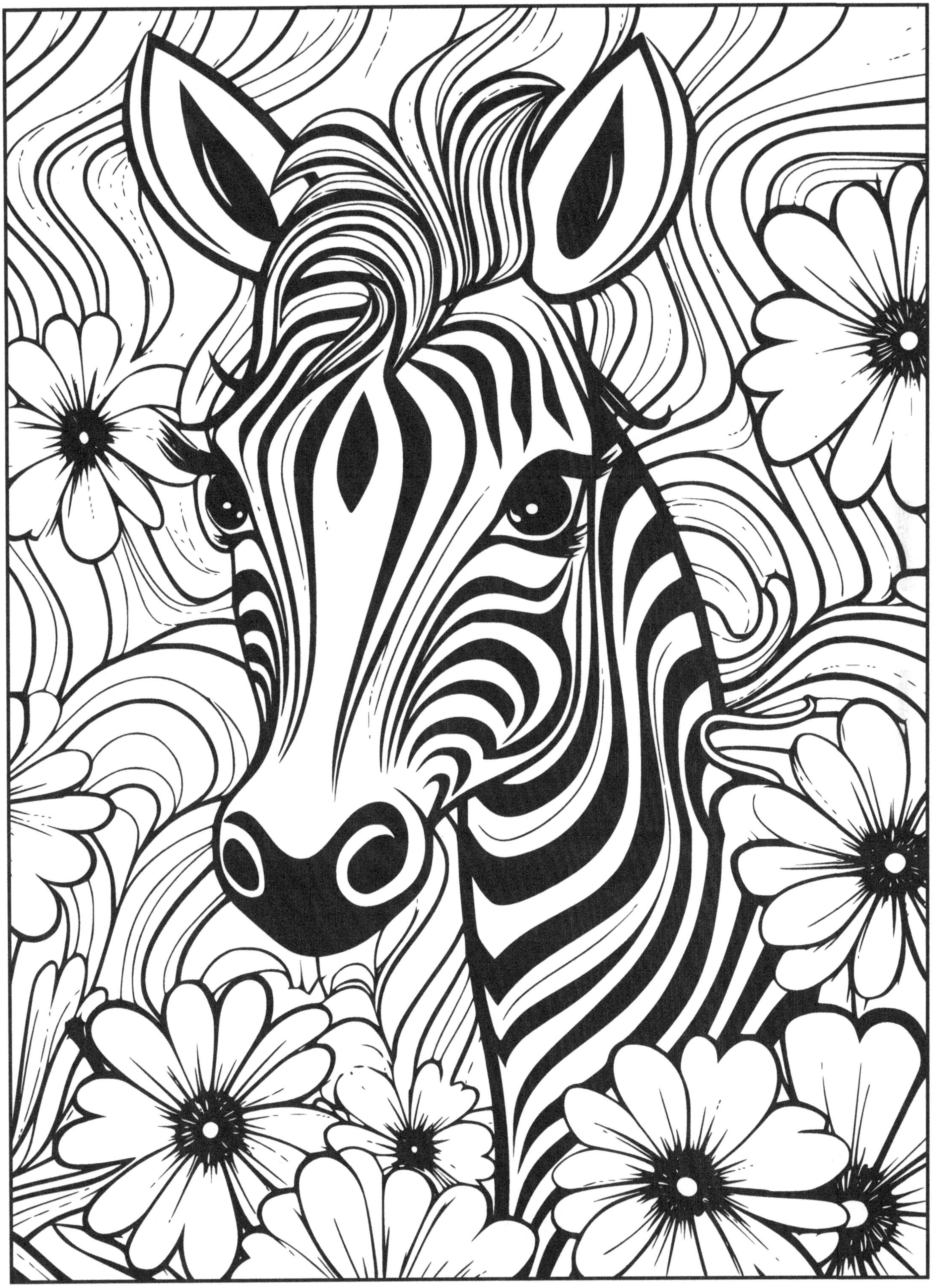

(This page intentionally left blank)

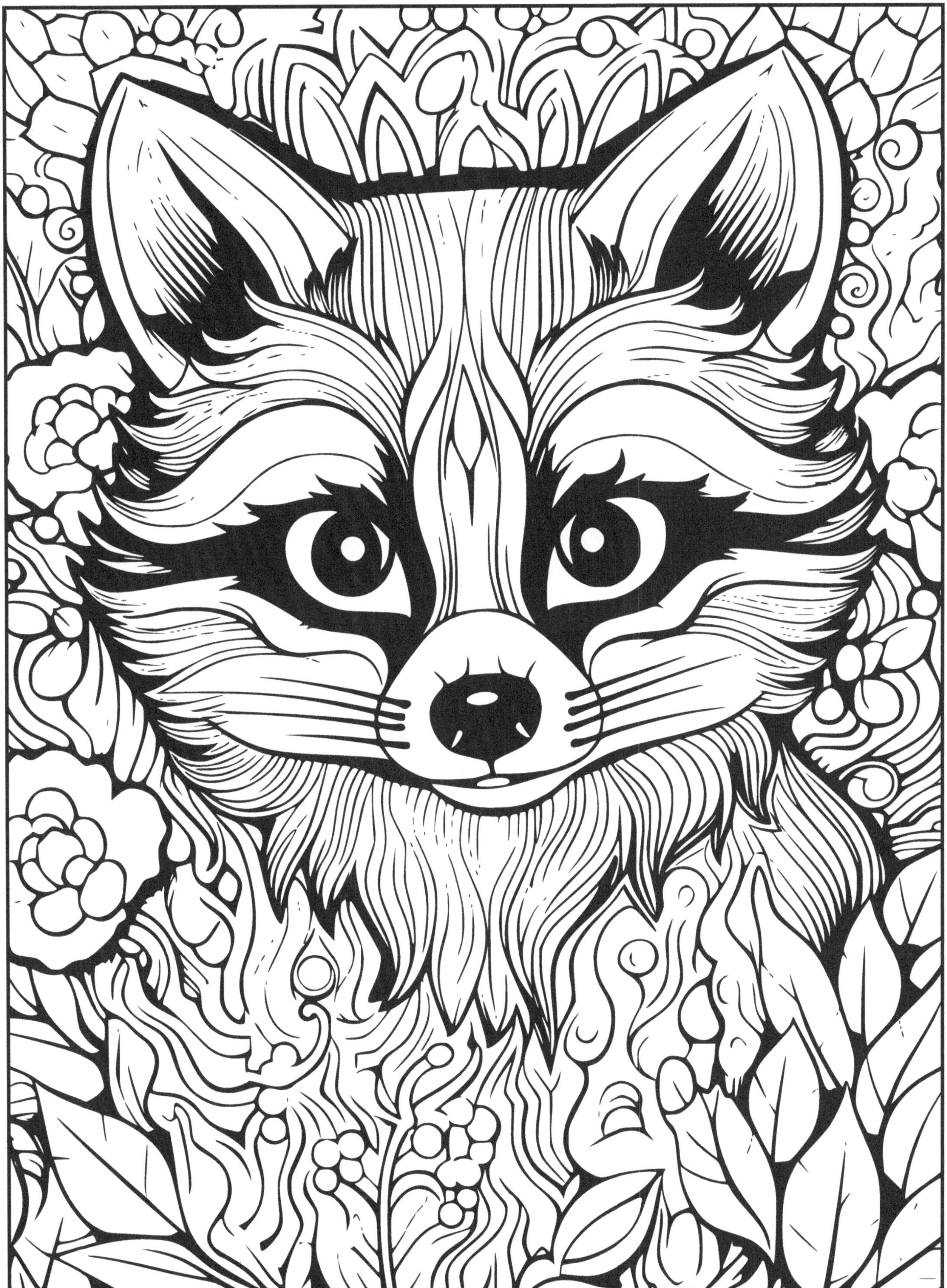

(This page intentionally left blank)

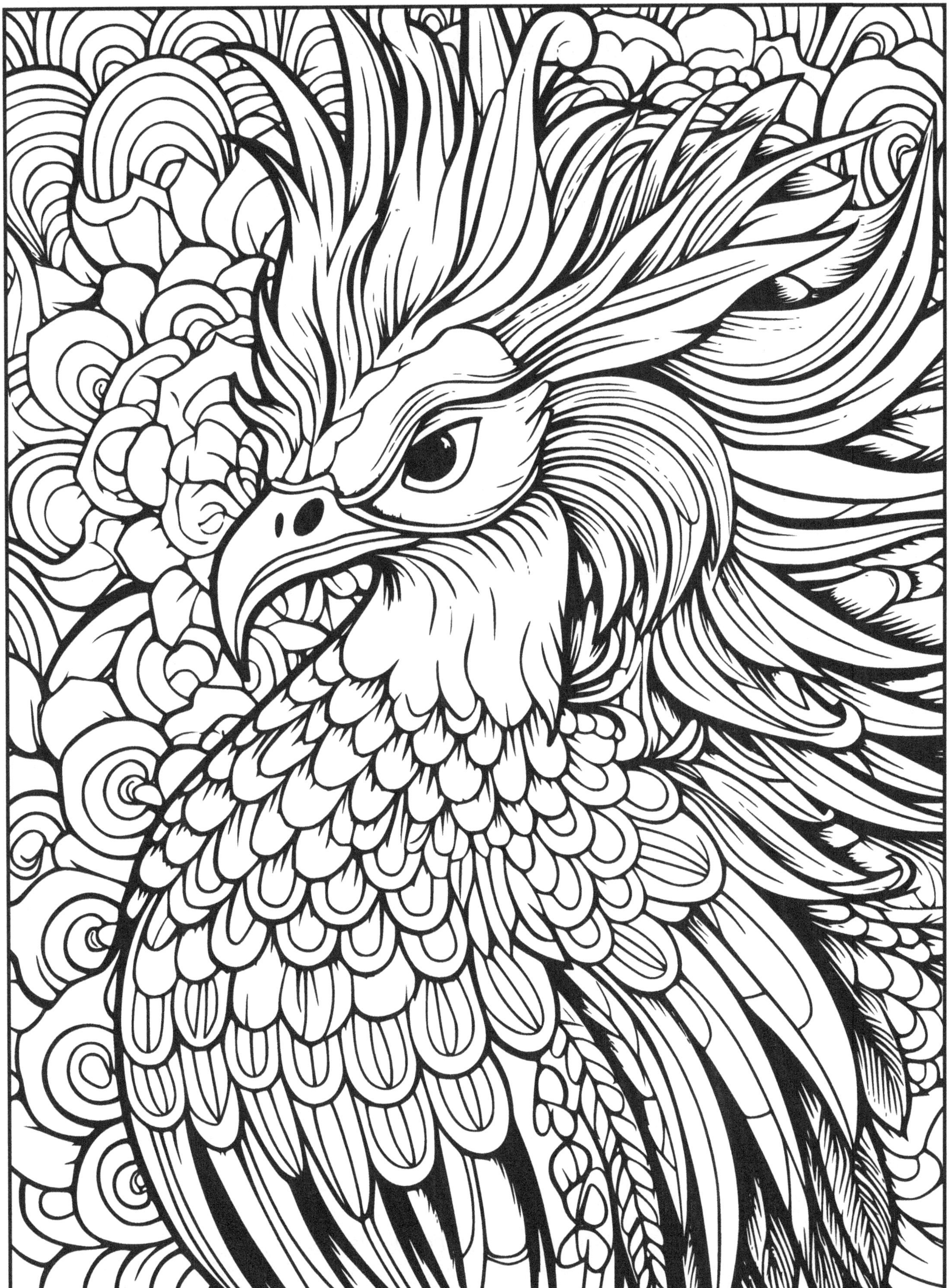

(This page intentionally left blank)

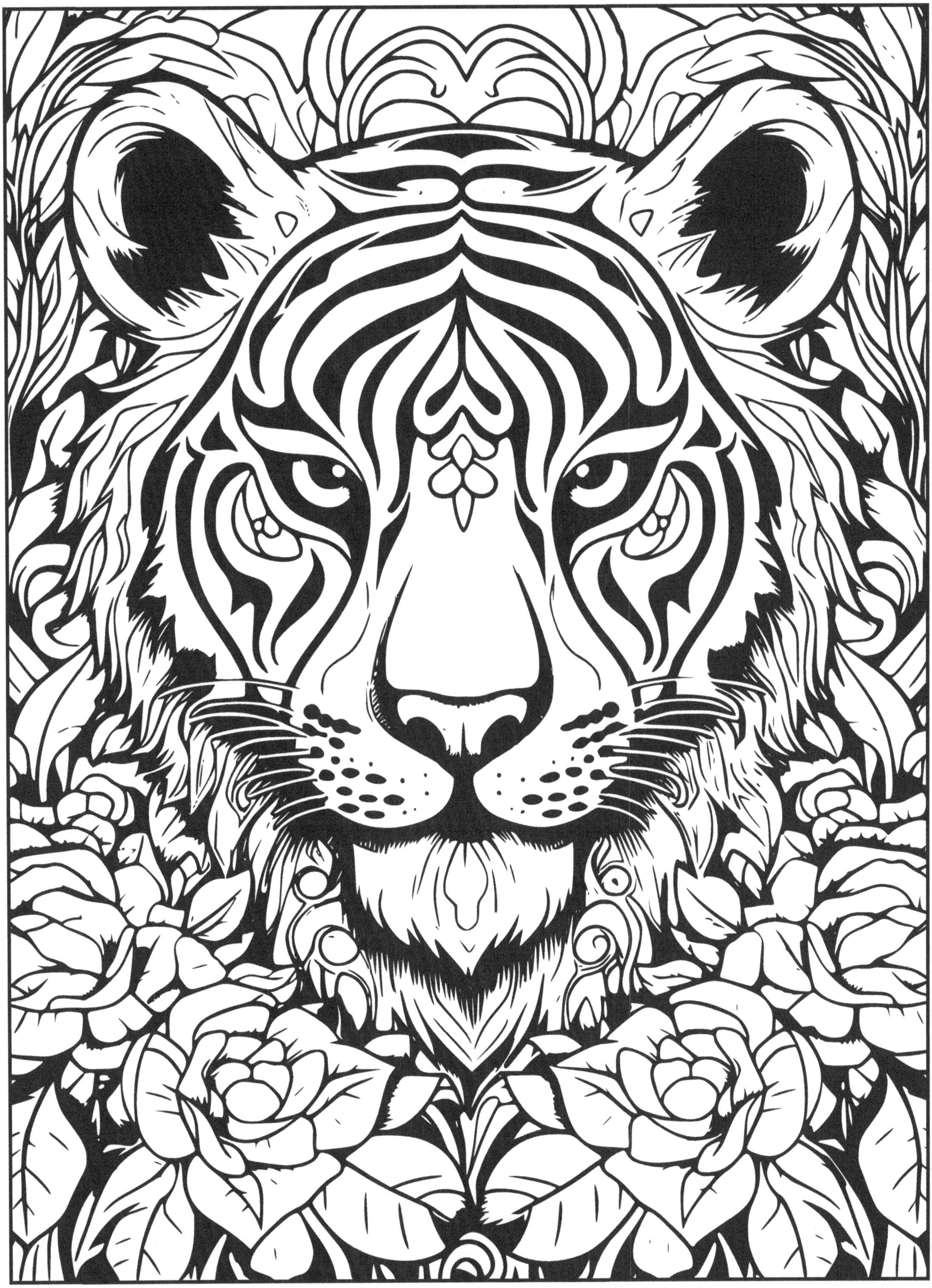

(This page intentionally left blank)

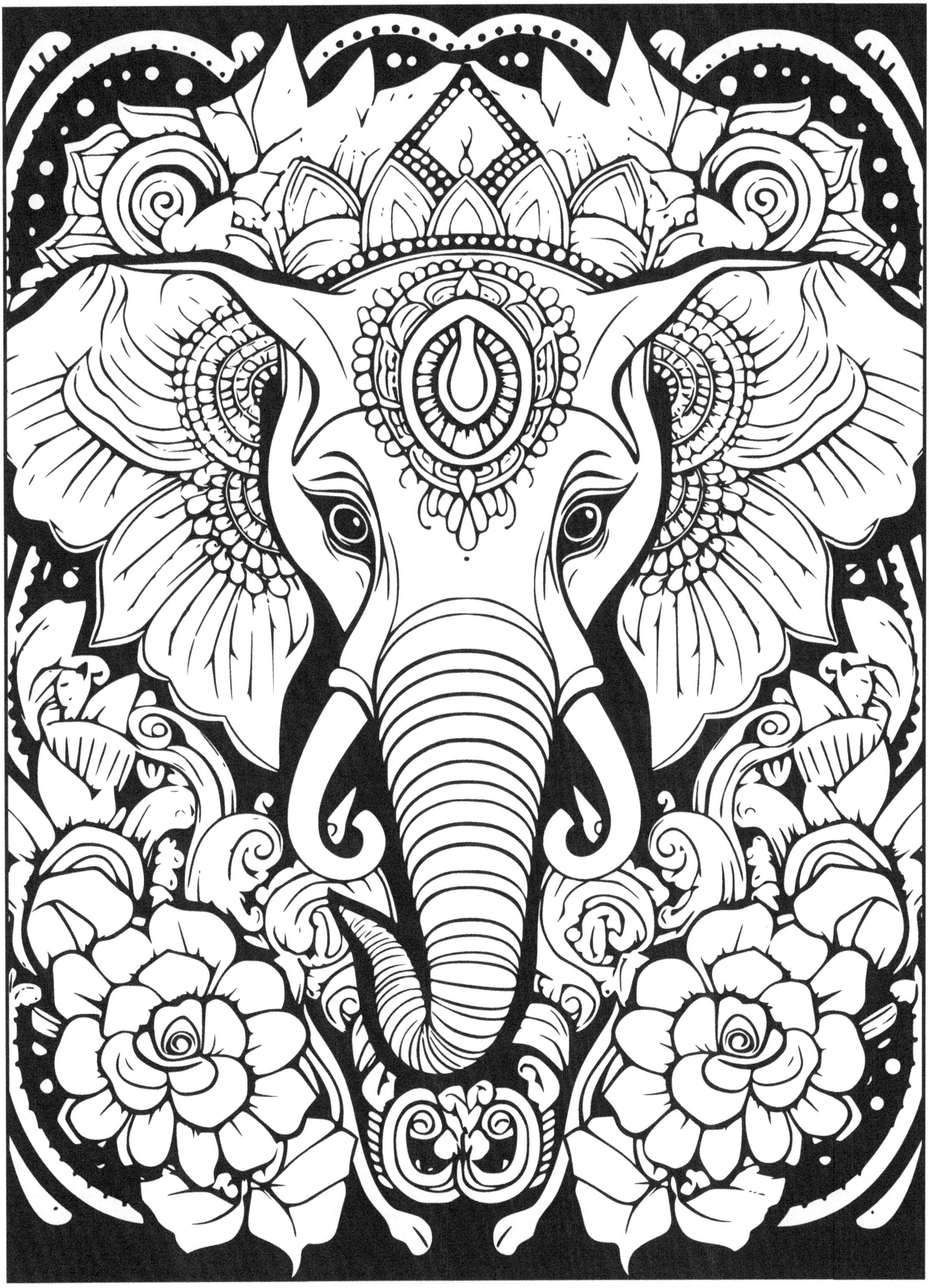

(This page intentionally left blank)

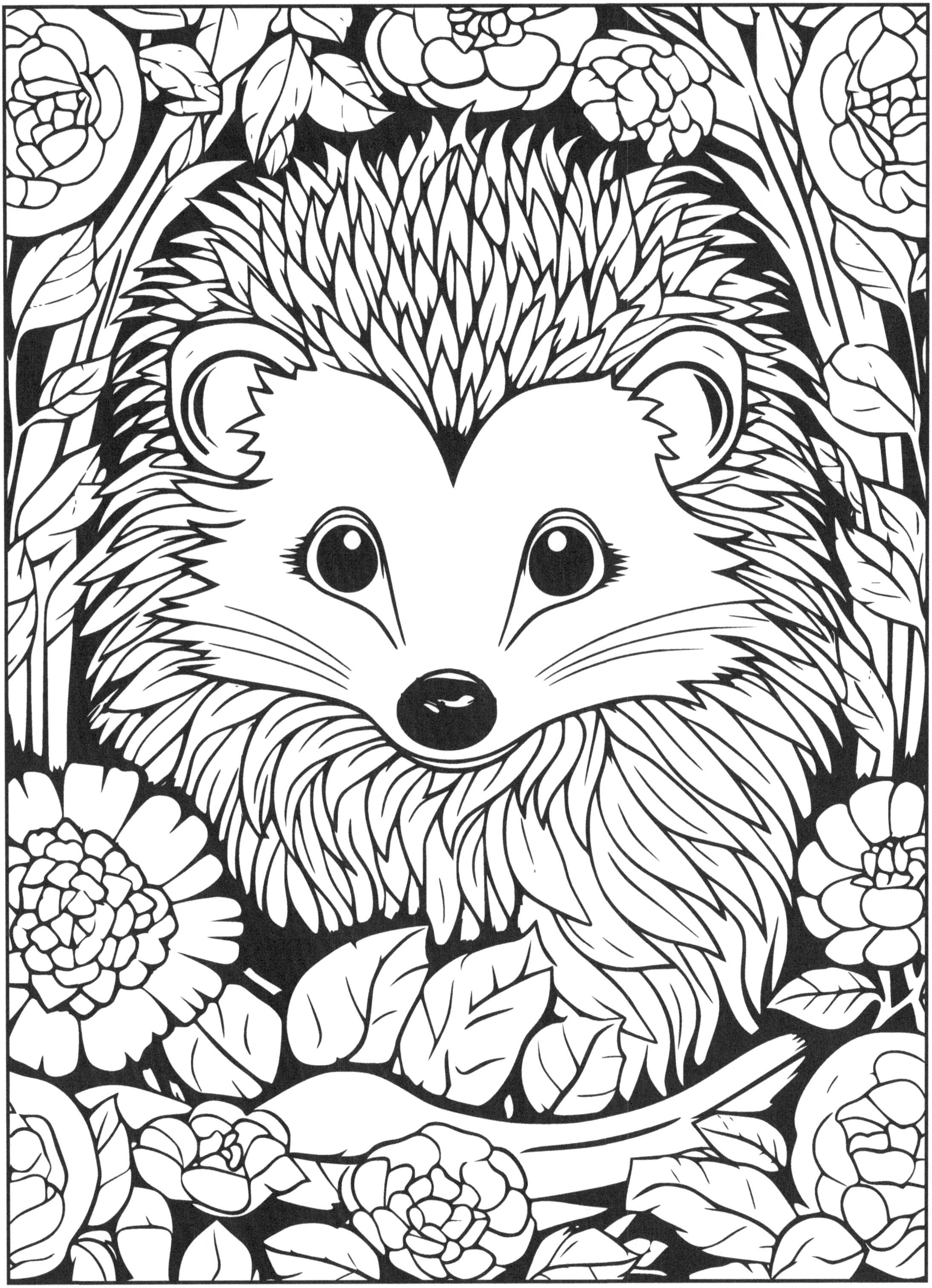

(This page intentionally left blank)

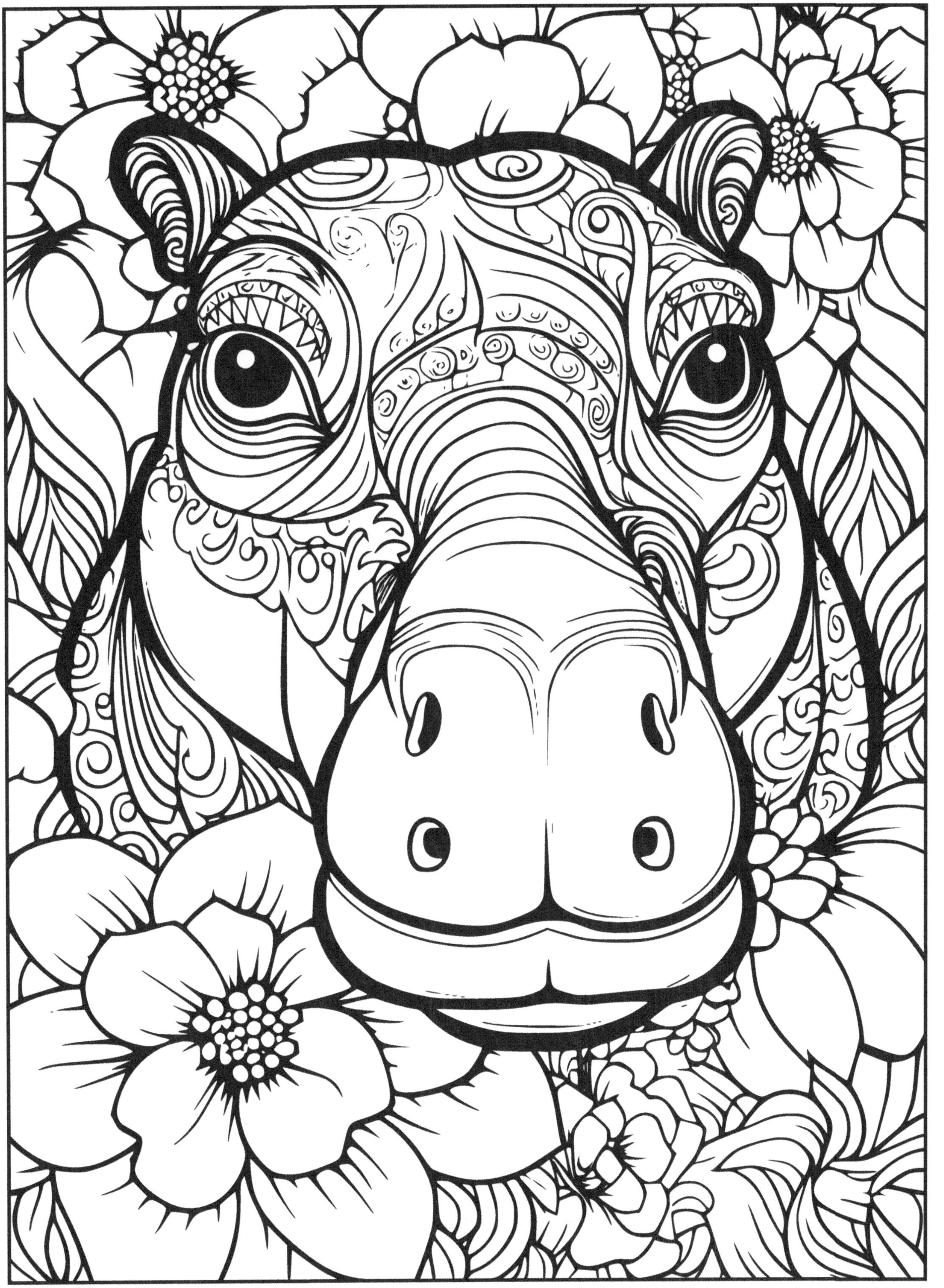

(This page intentionally left blank)

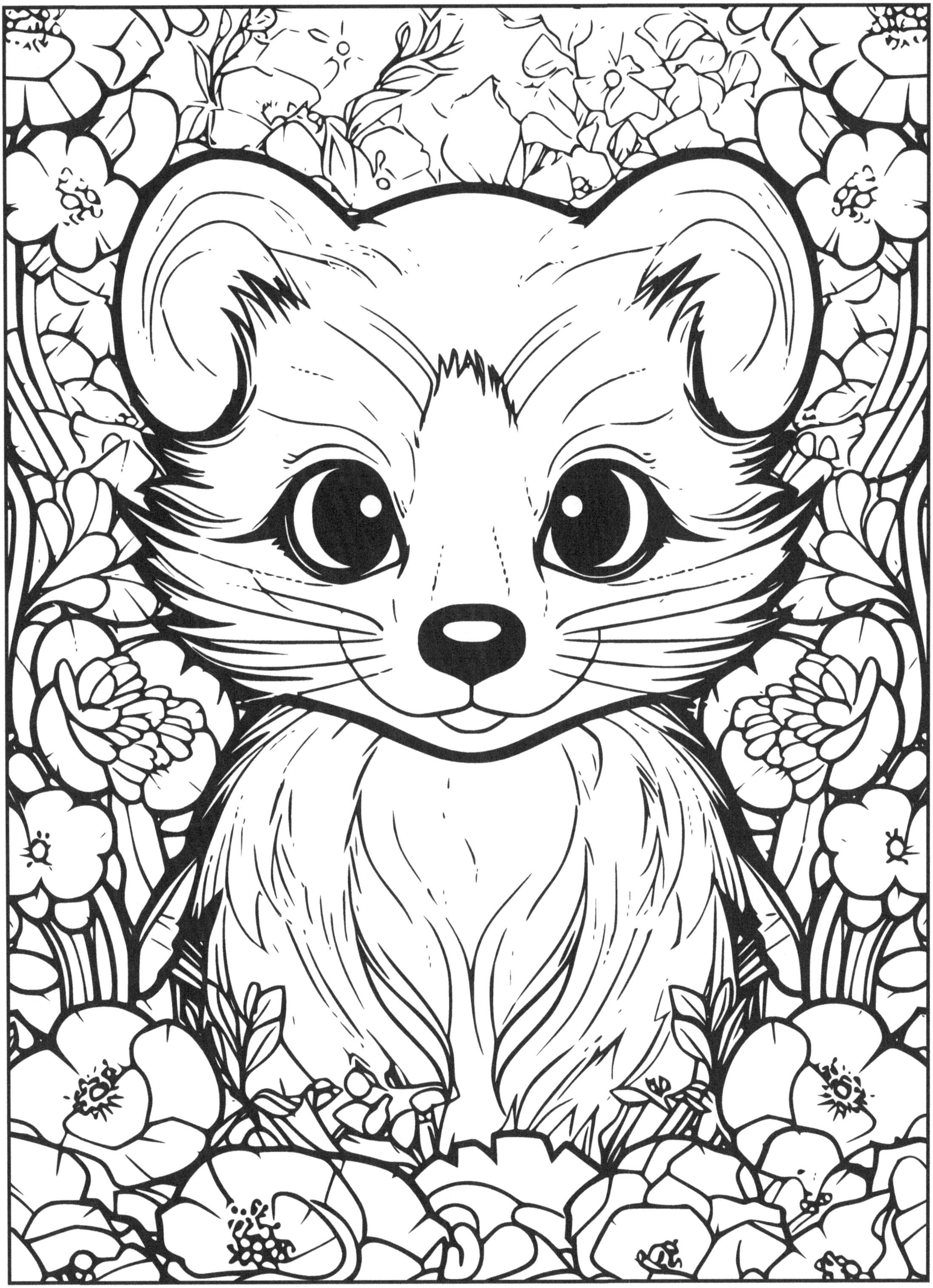

(This page intentionally left blank)

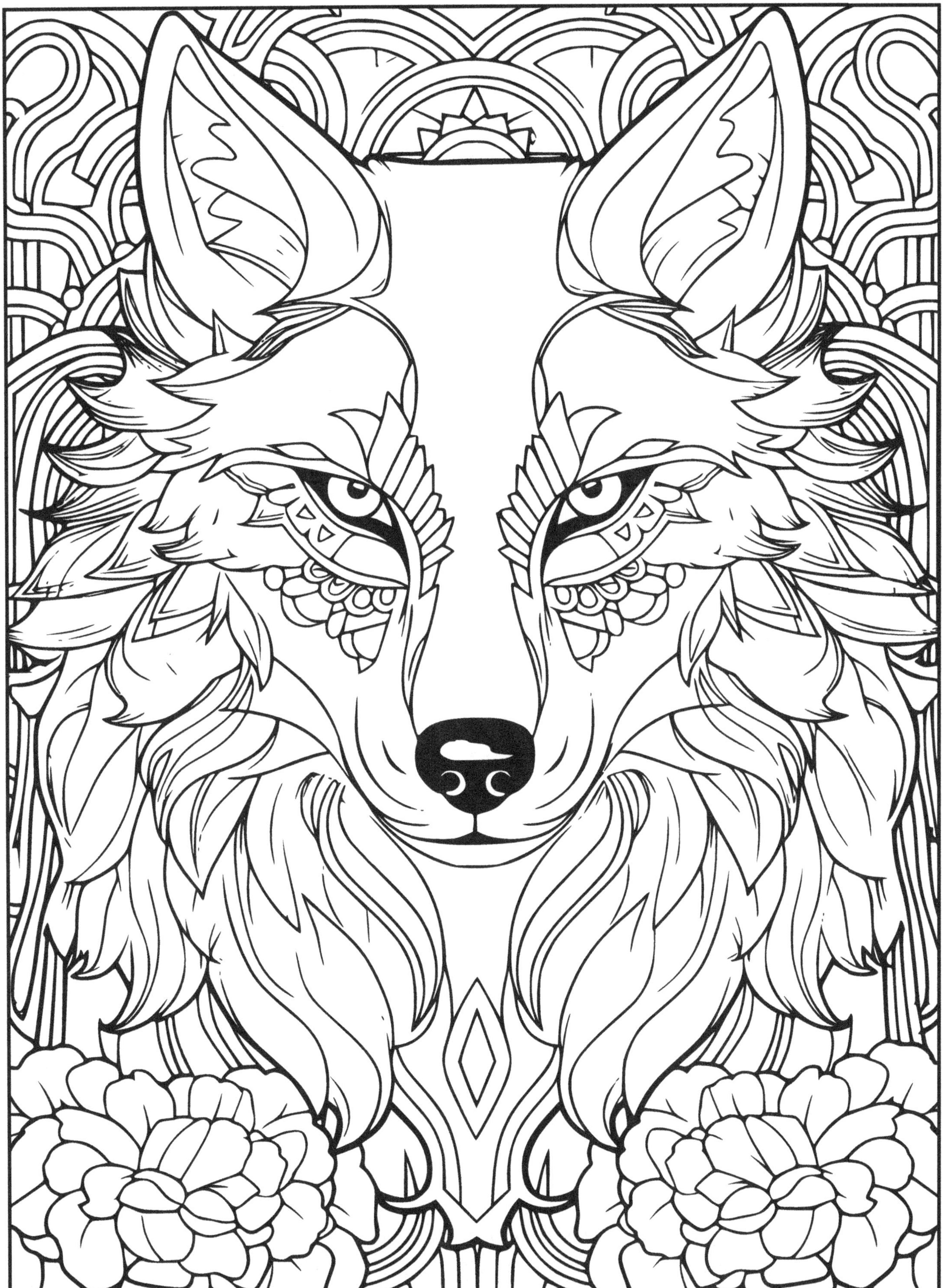

(This page intentionally left blank)

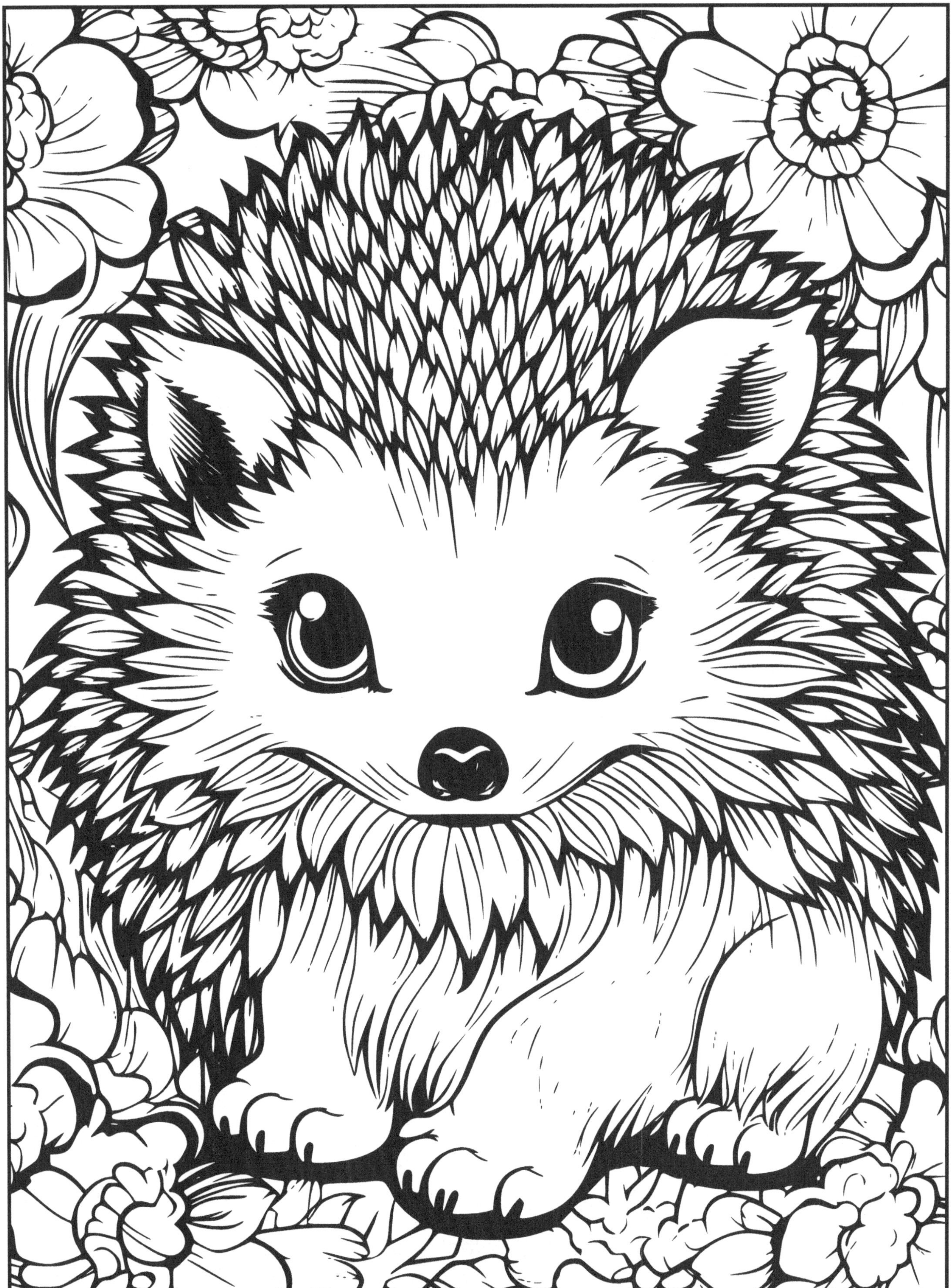

(This page intentionally left blank)

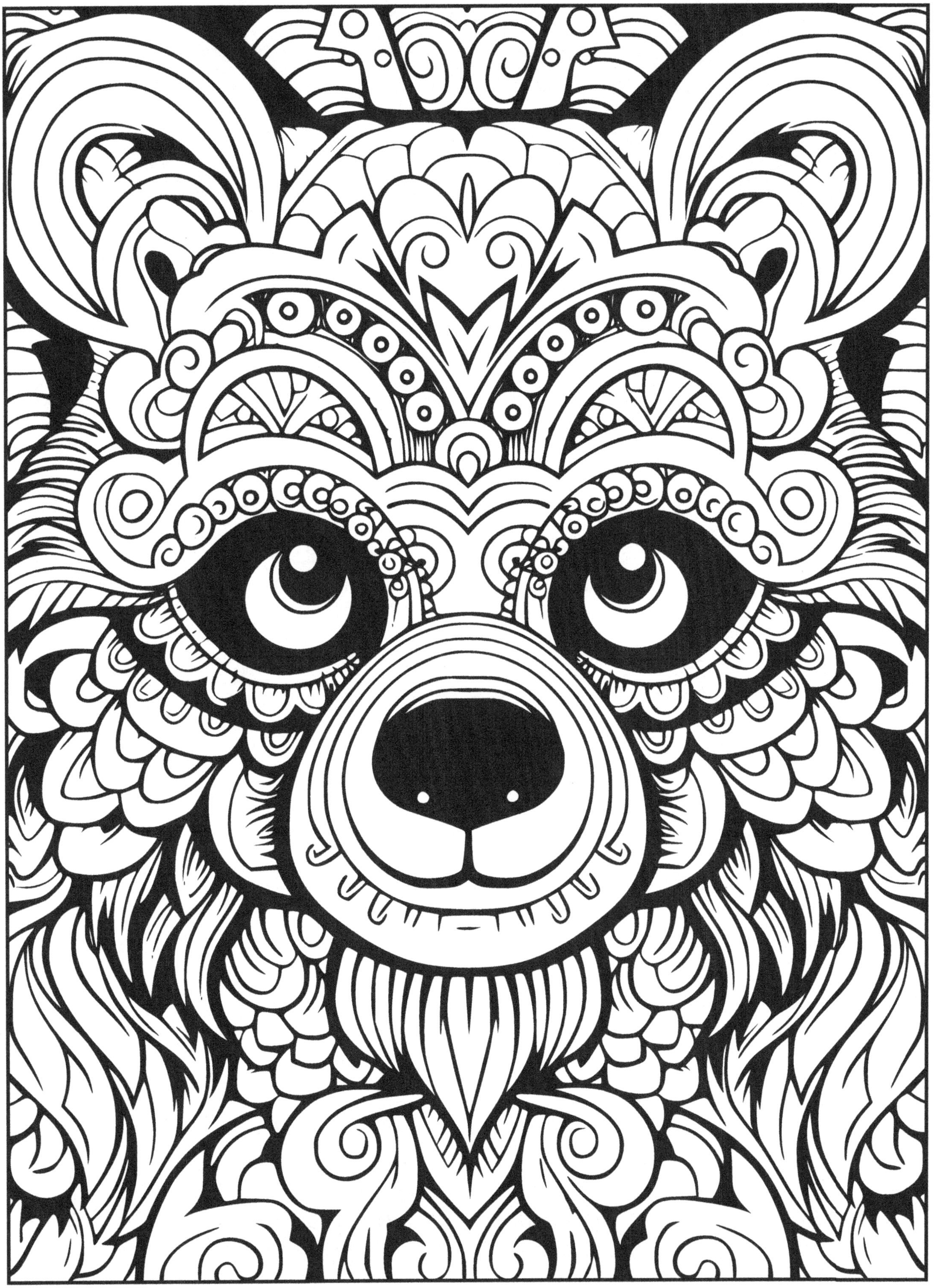

(This page intentionally left blank)

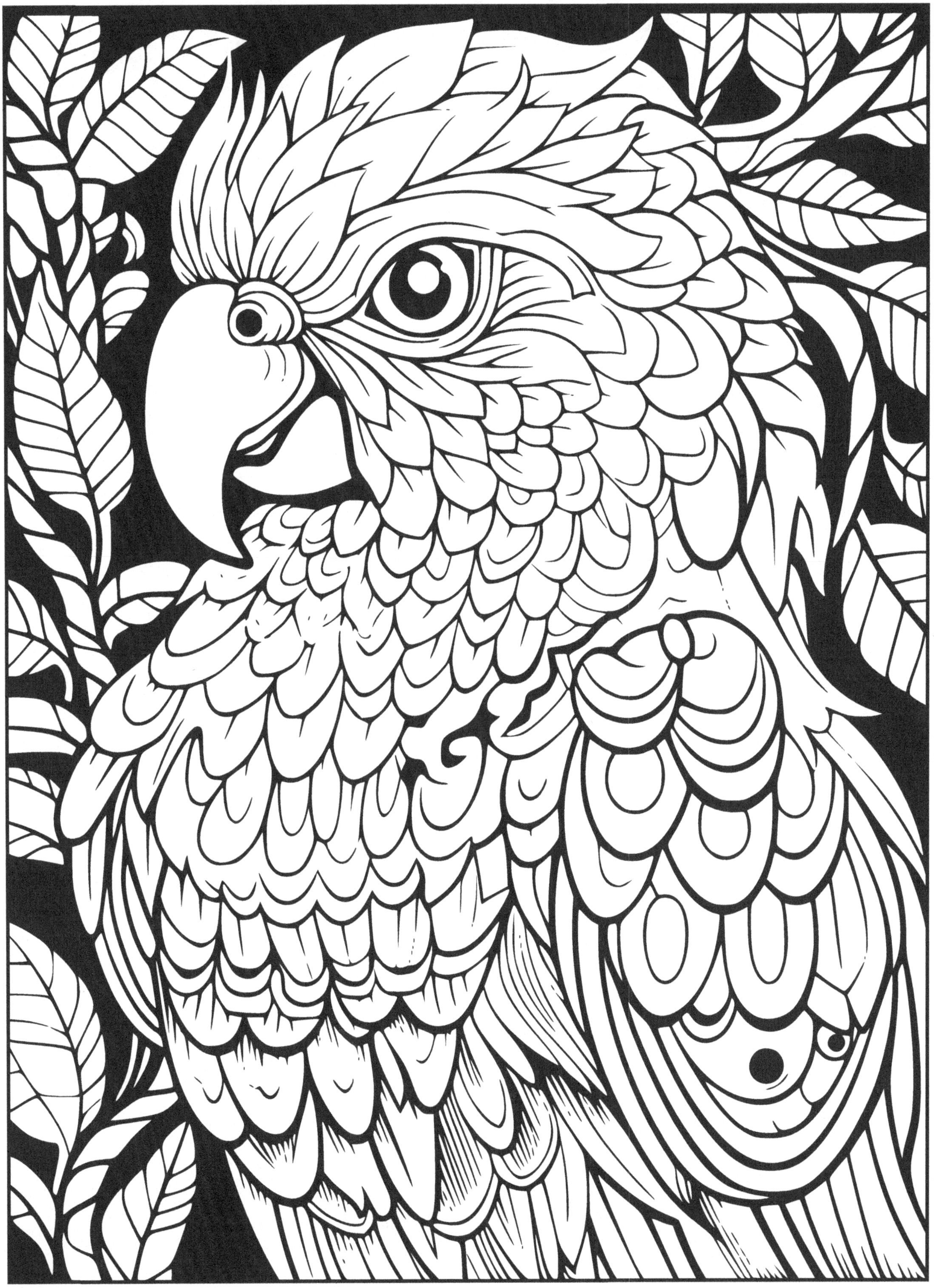

(This page intentionally left blank)

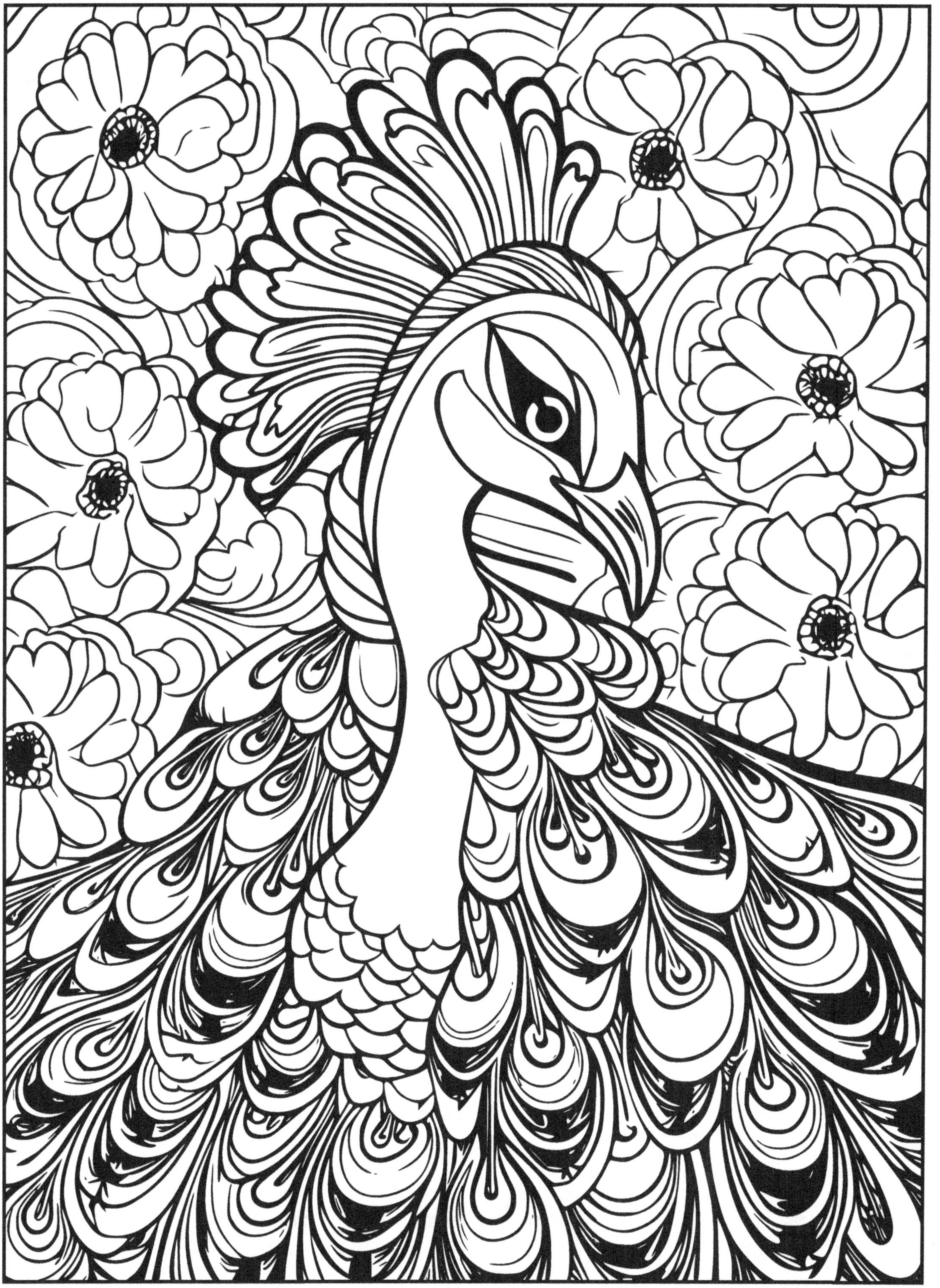

(This page intentionally left blank)

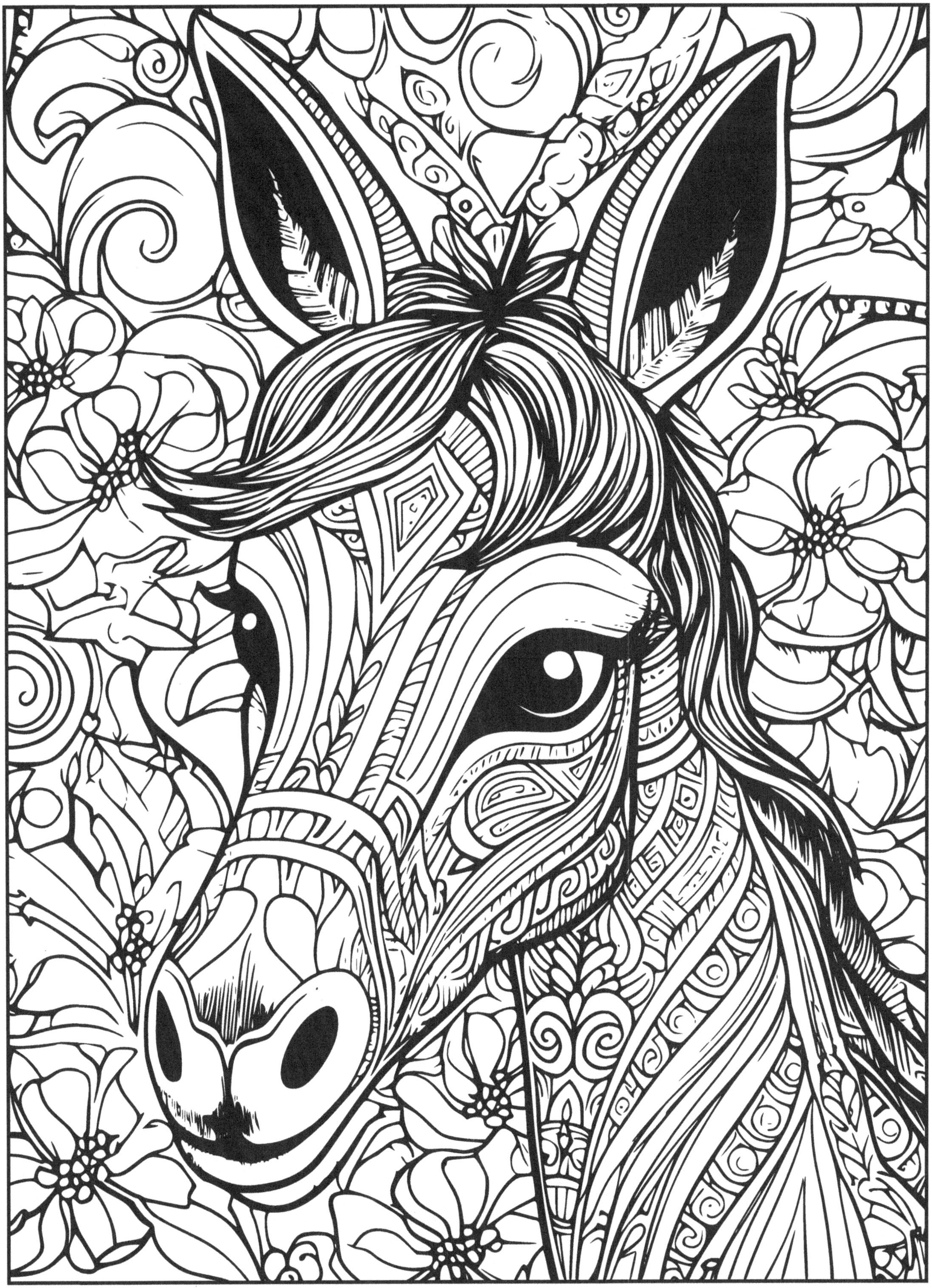

(This page intentionally left blank)

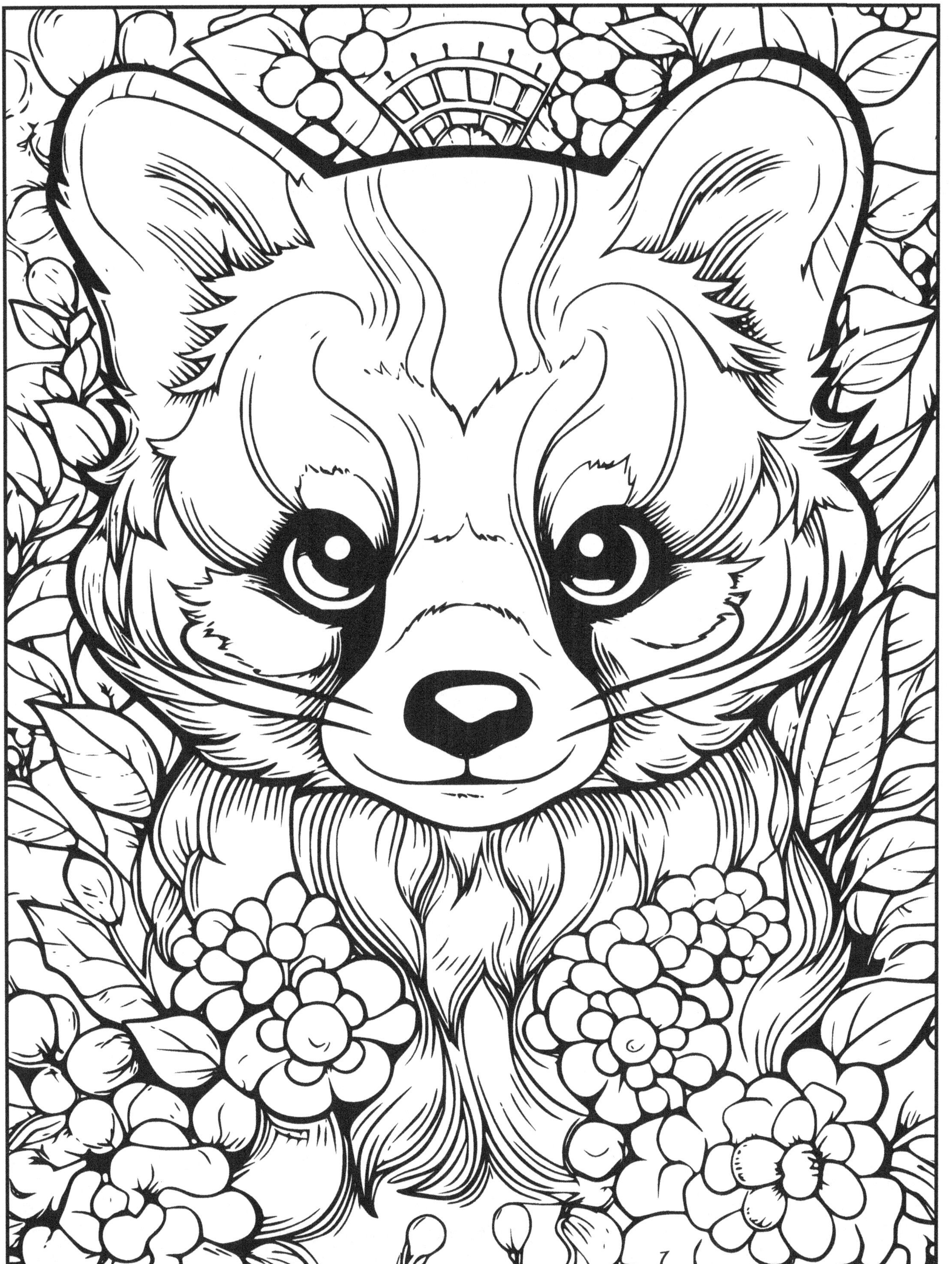

(This page intentionally left blank)

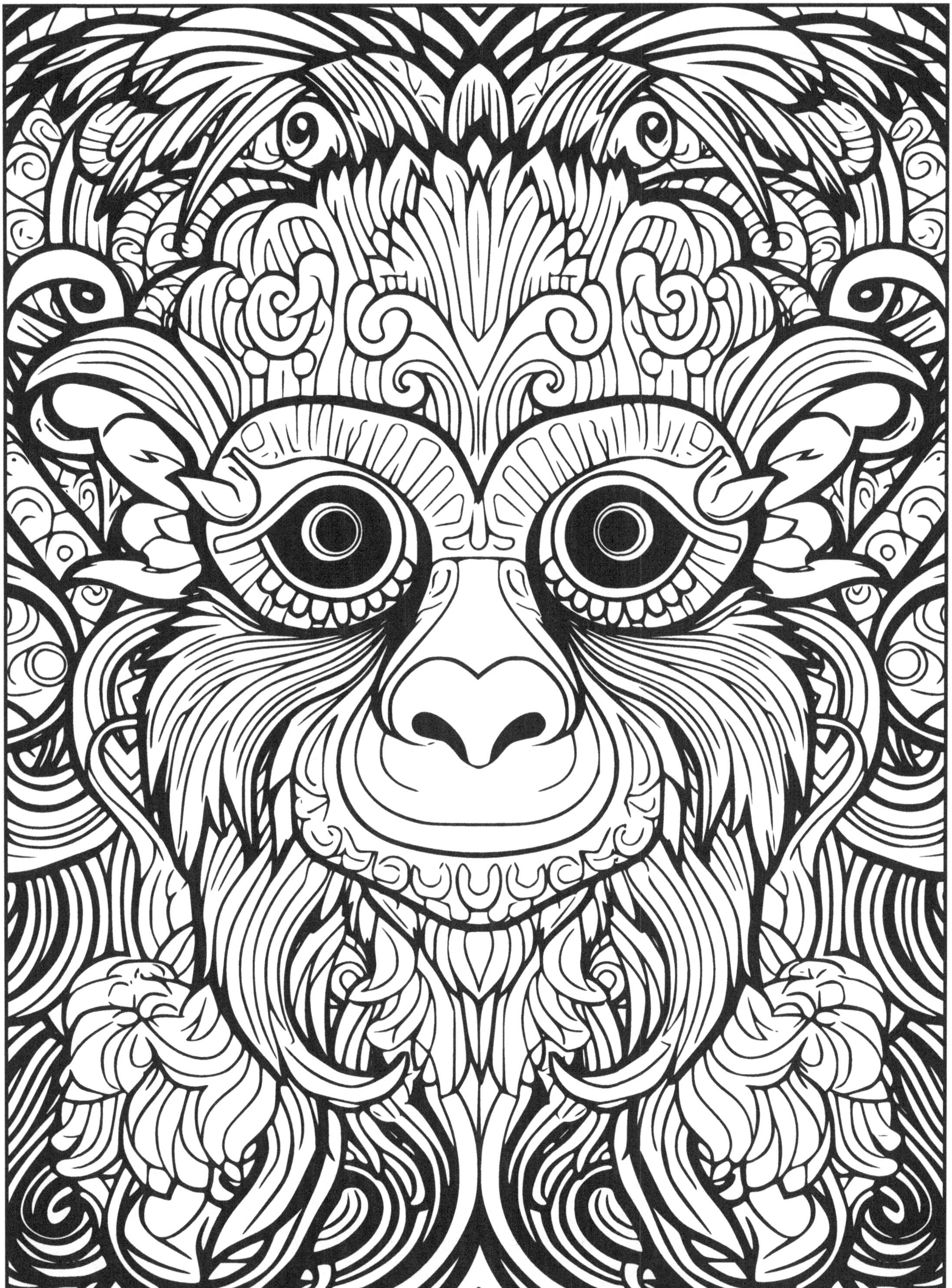

(This page intentionally left blank)

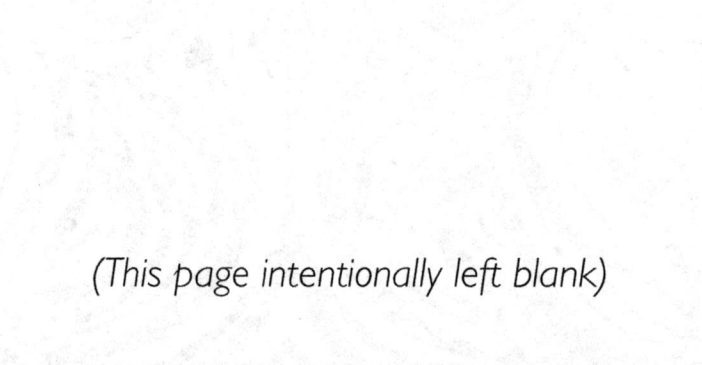

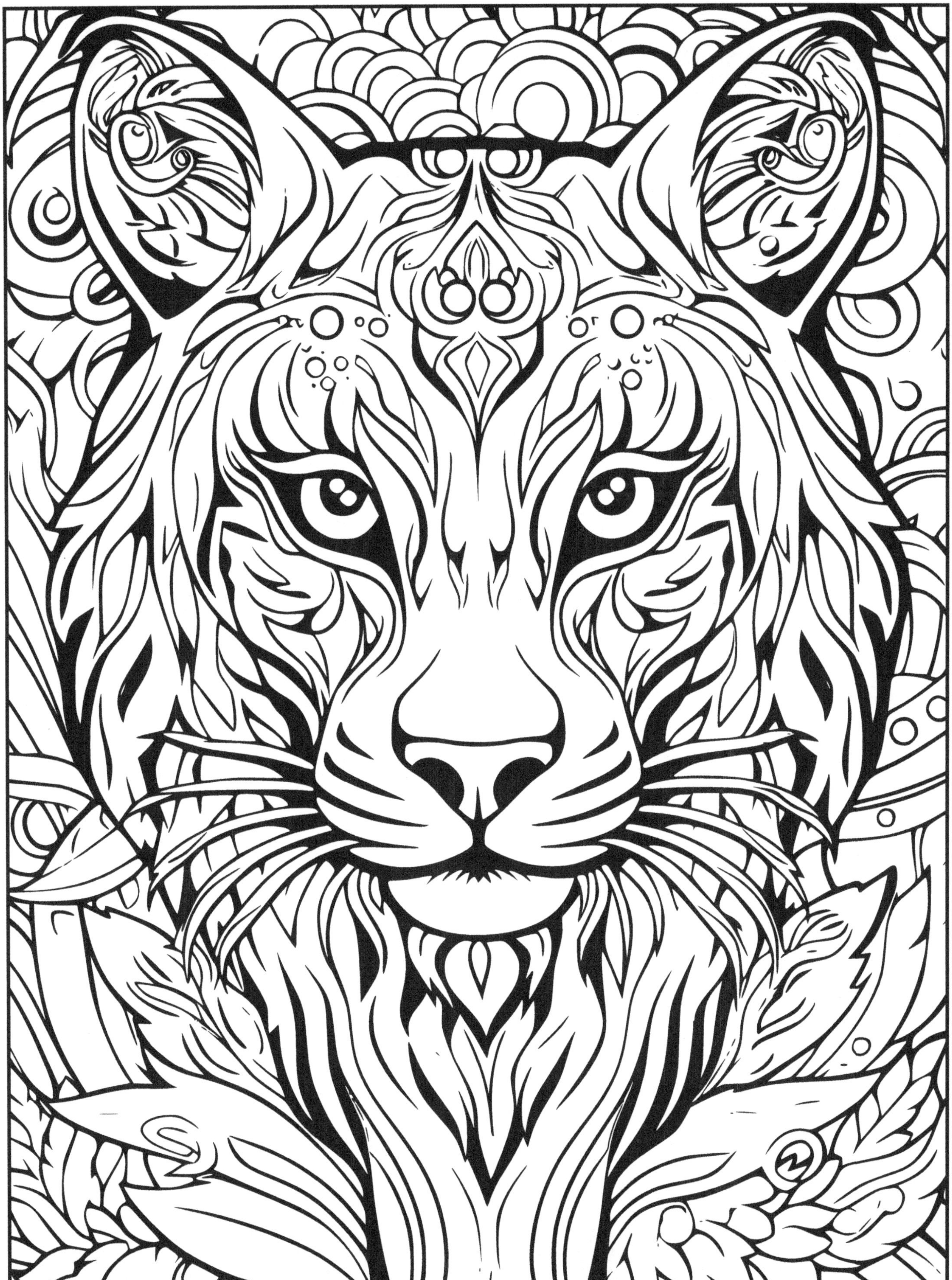

(This page intentionally left blank)

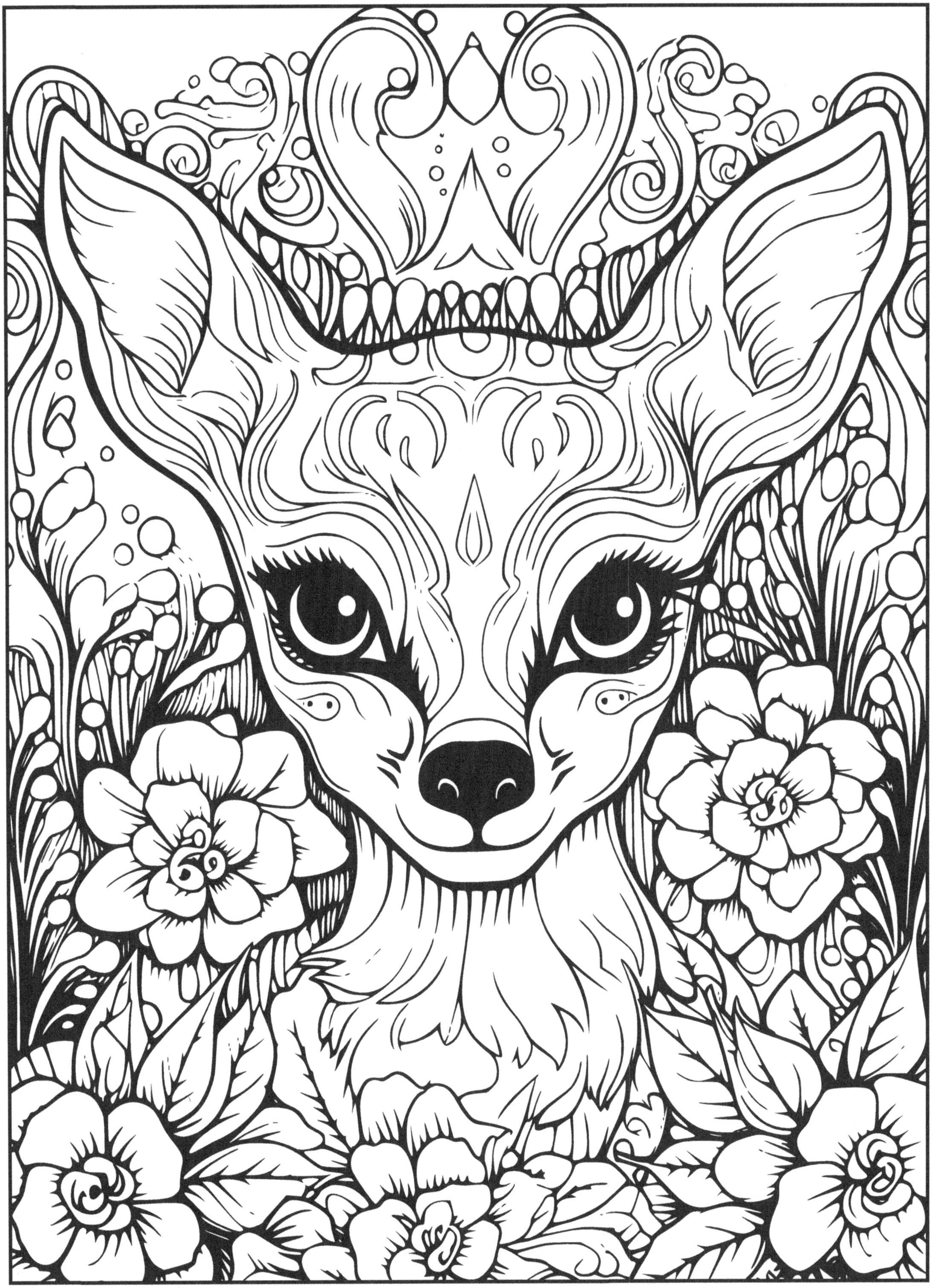

(This page intentionally left blank)

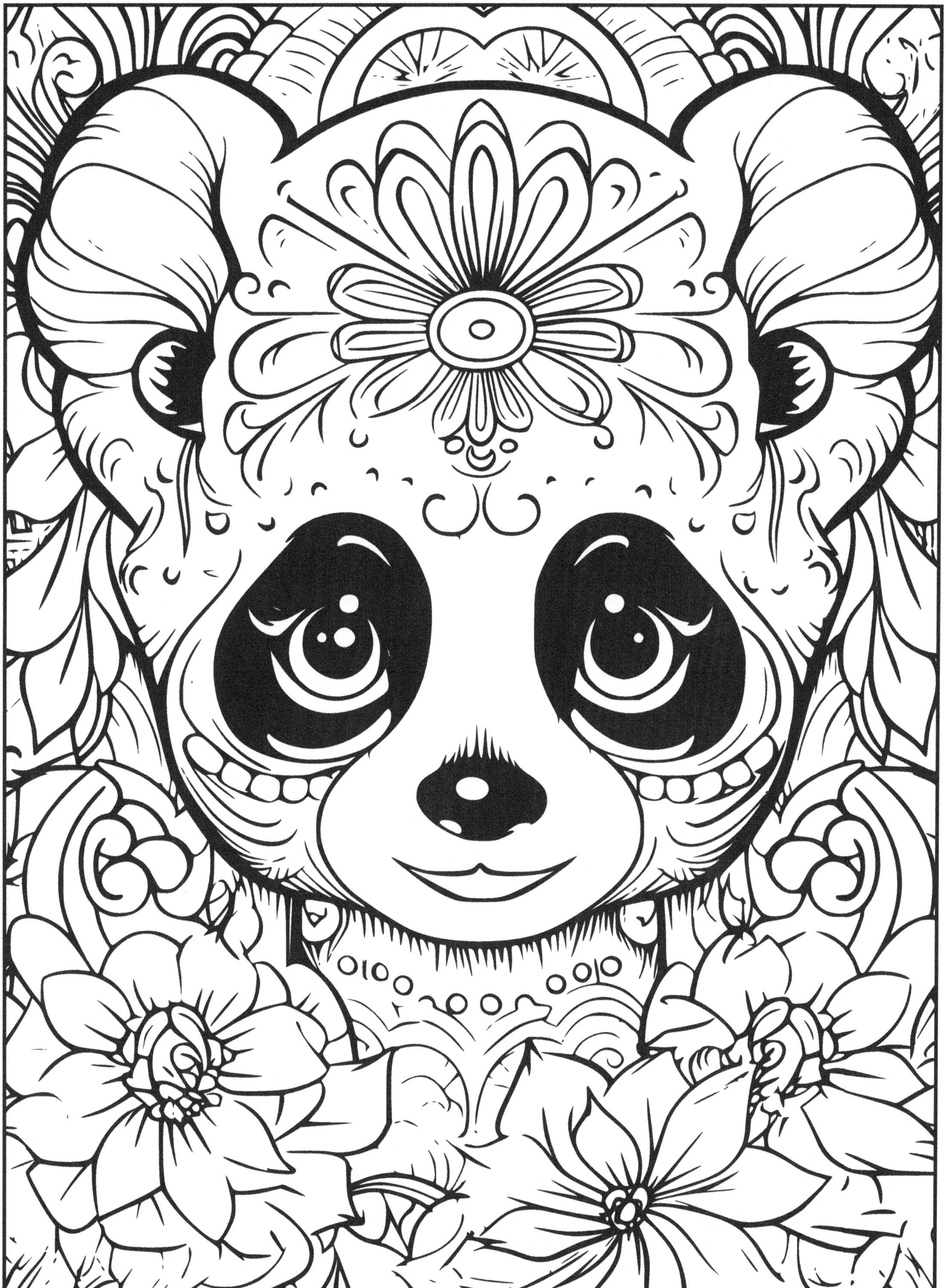

(This page intentionally left blank)

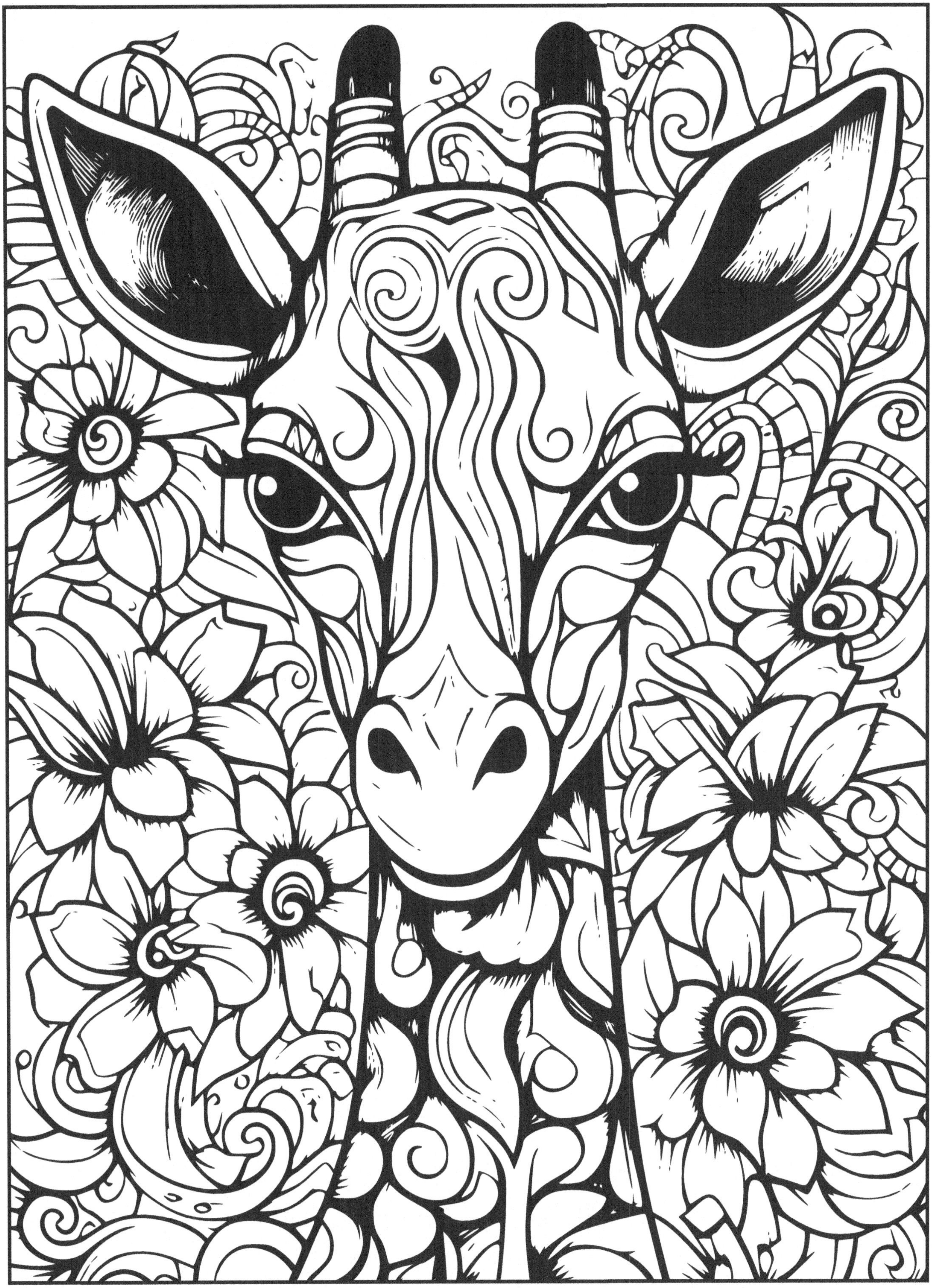

(This page intentionally left blank)

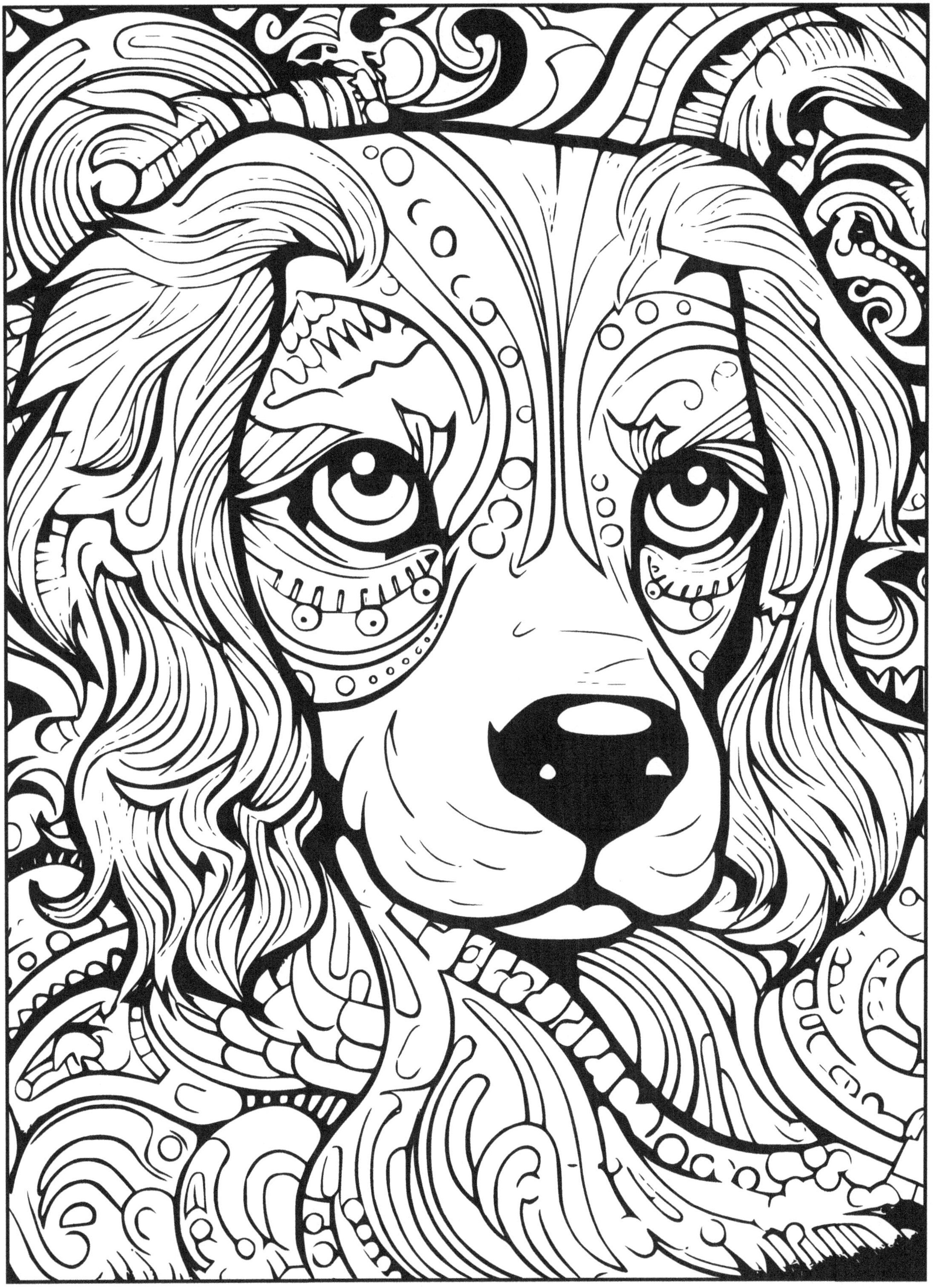

(This page intentionally left blank)

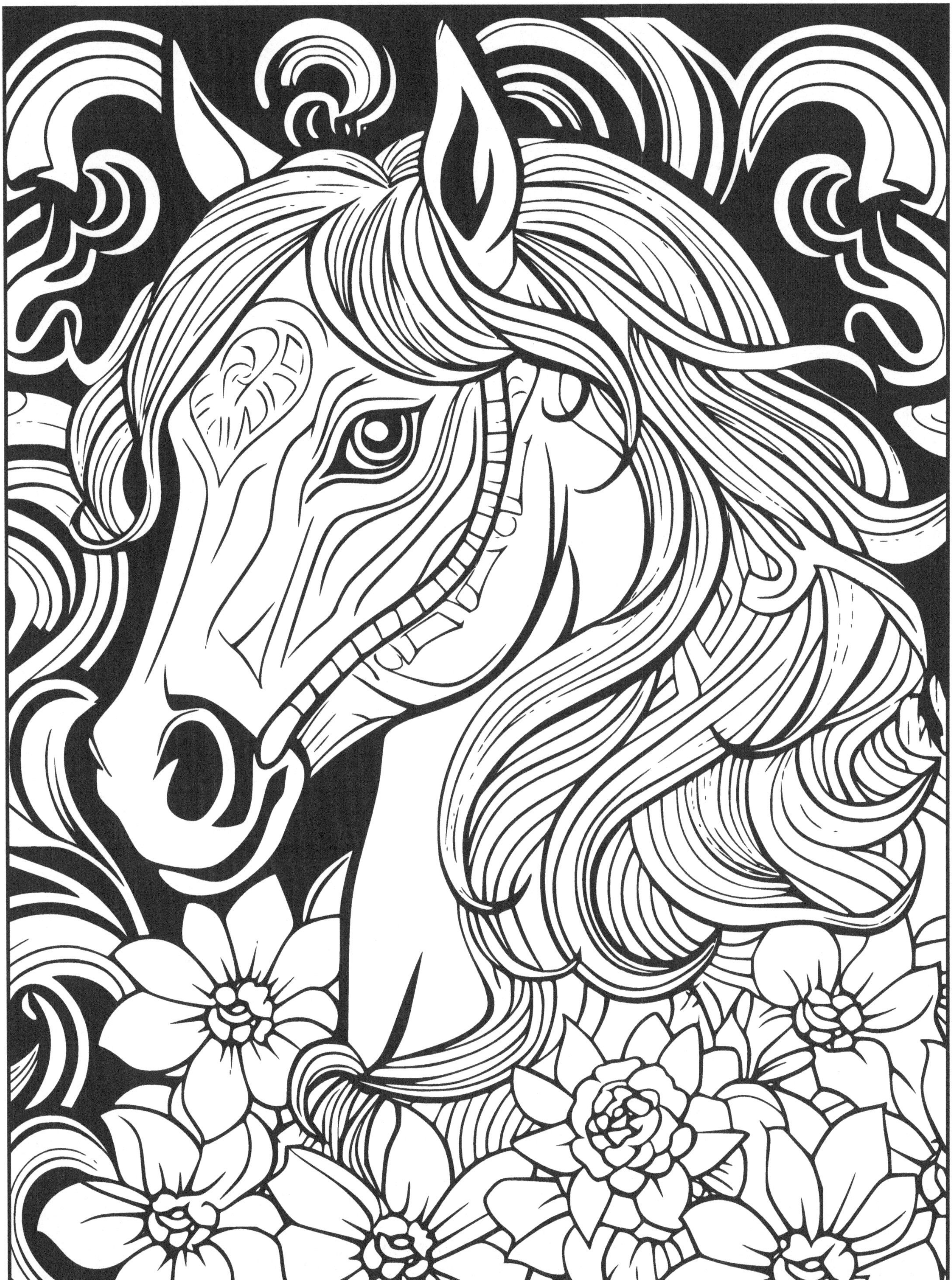

(This page intentionally left blank)

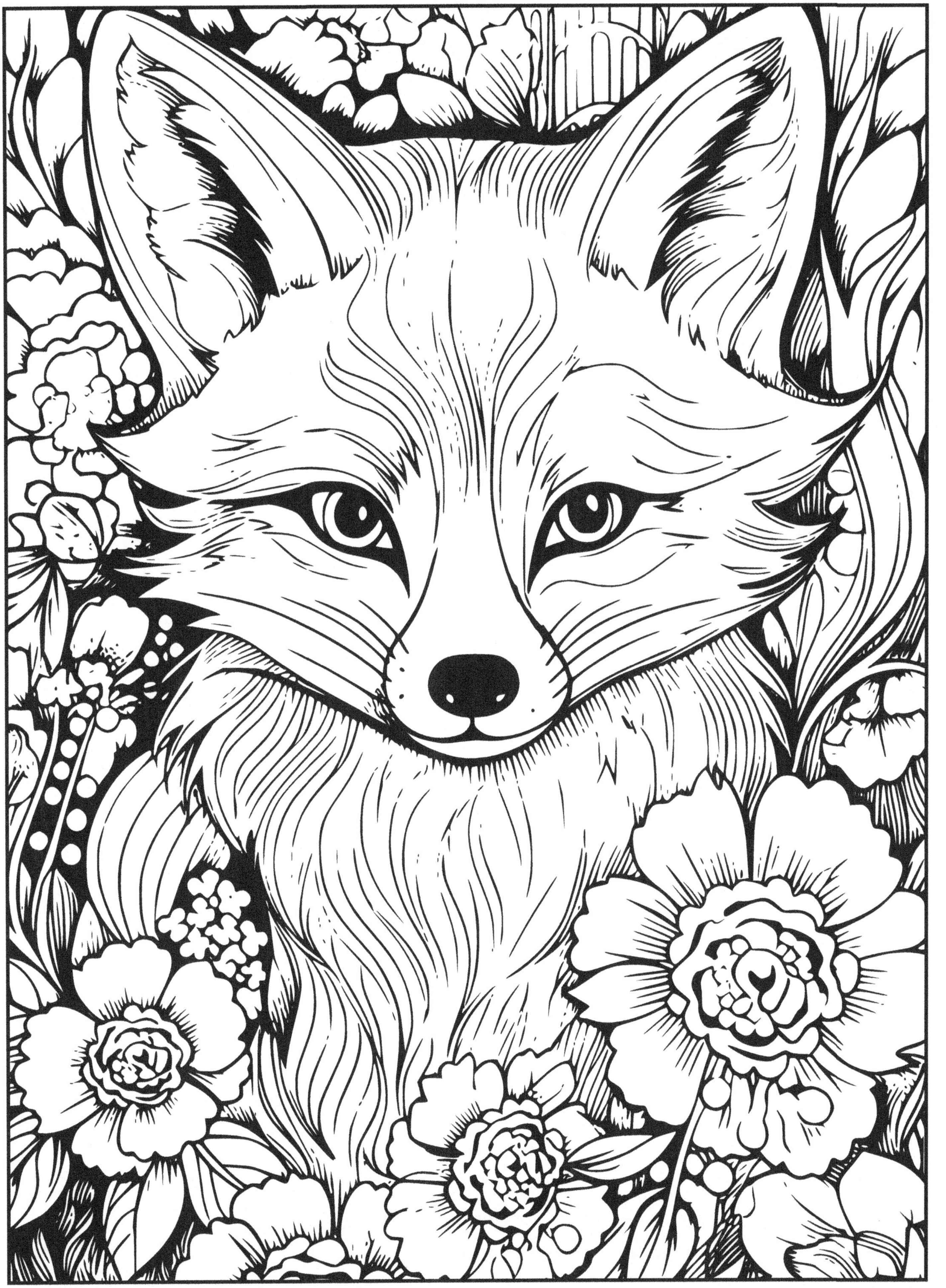

(This page intentionally left blank)

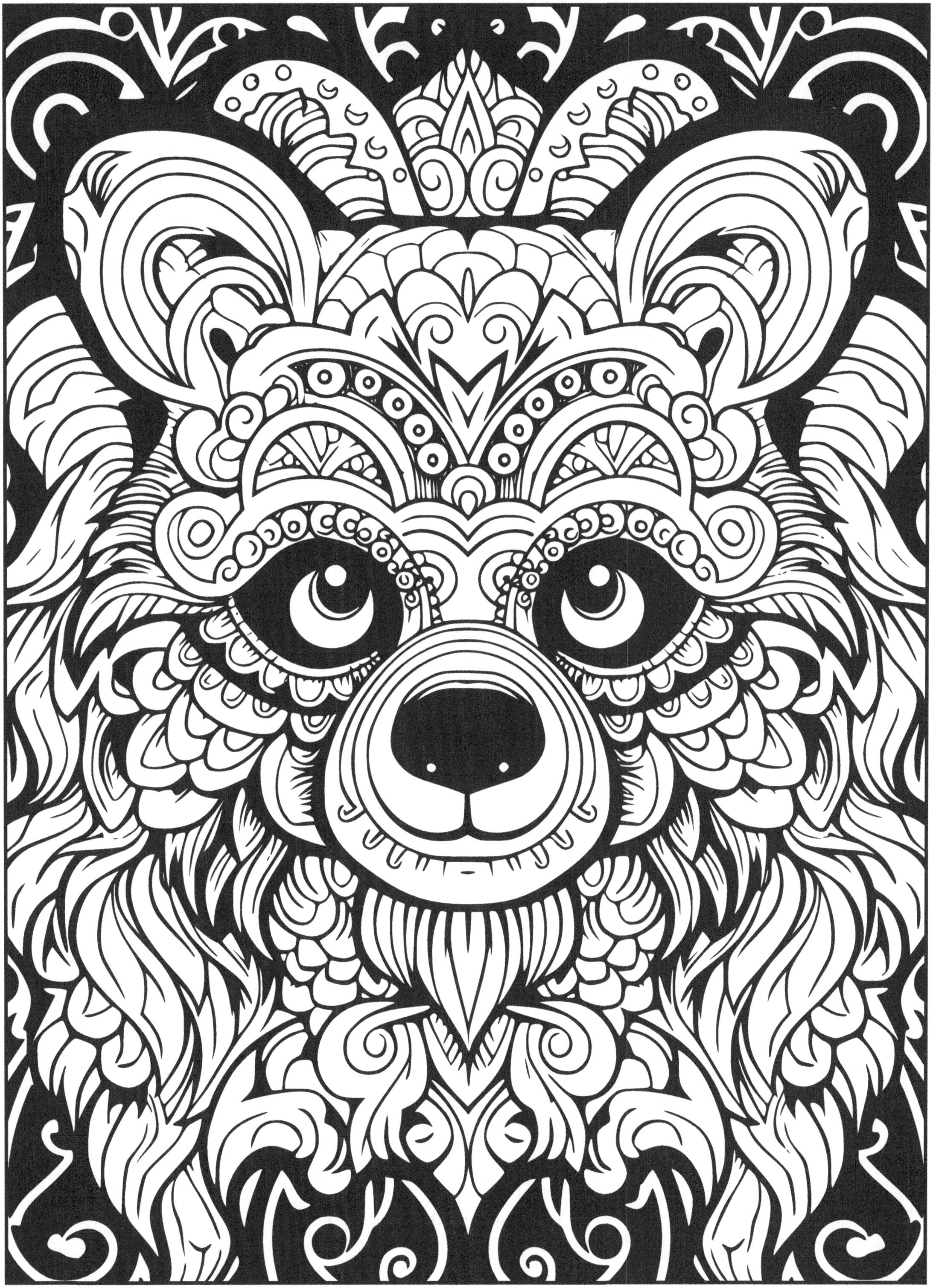

(This page intentionally left blank)

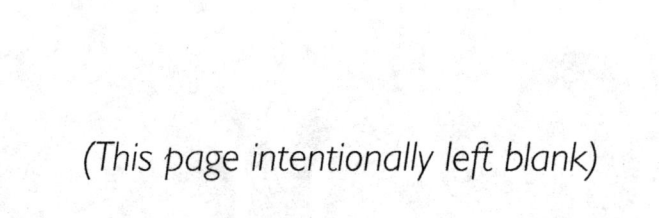

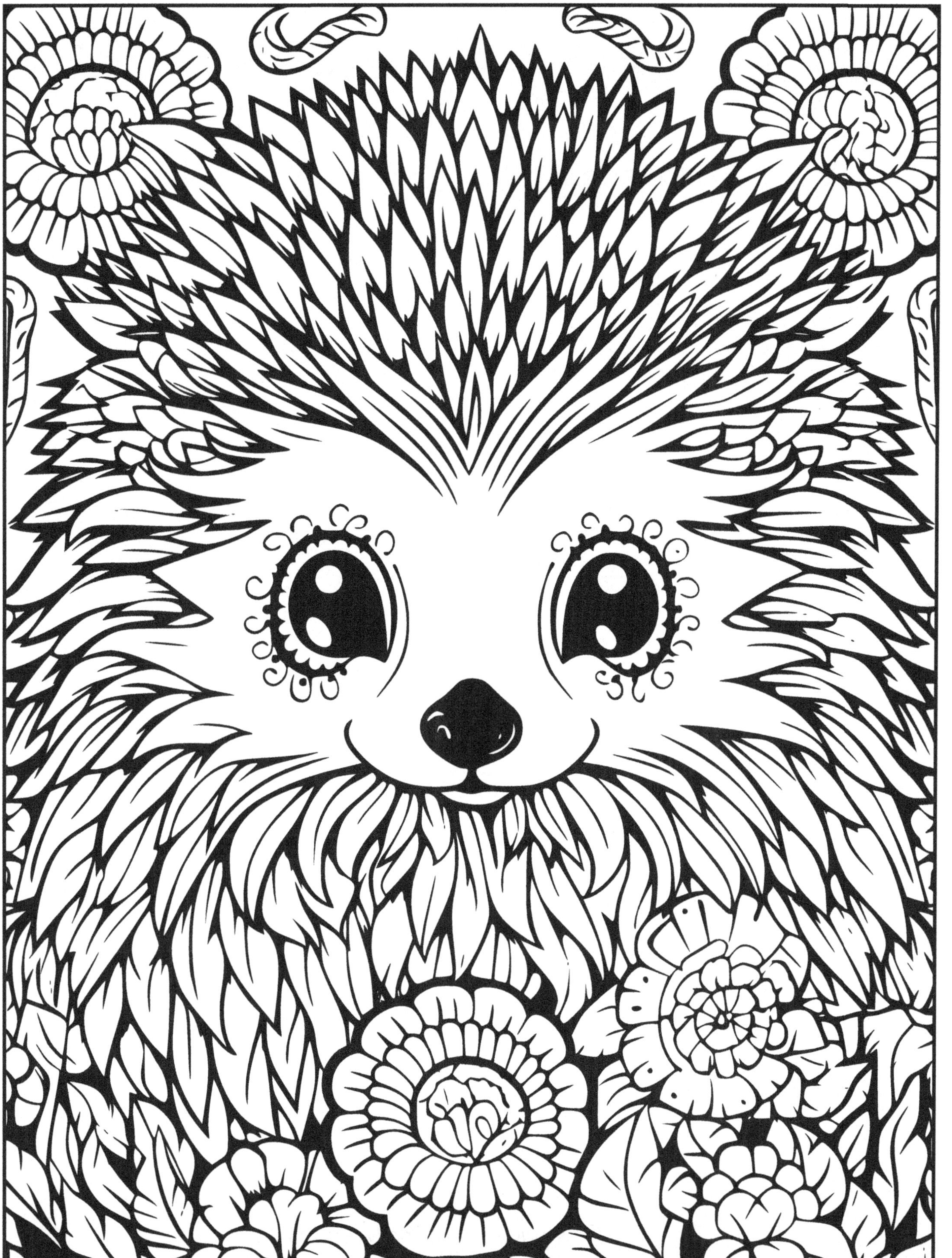

(This page intentionally left blank)

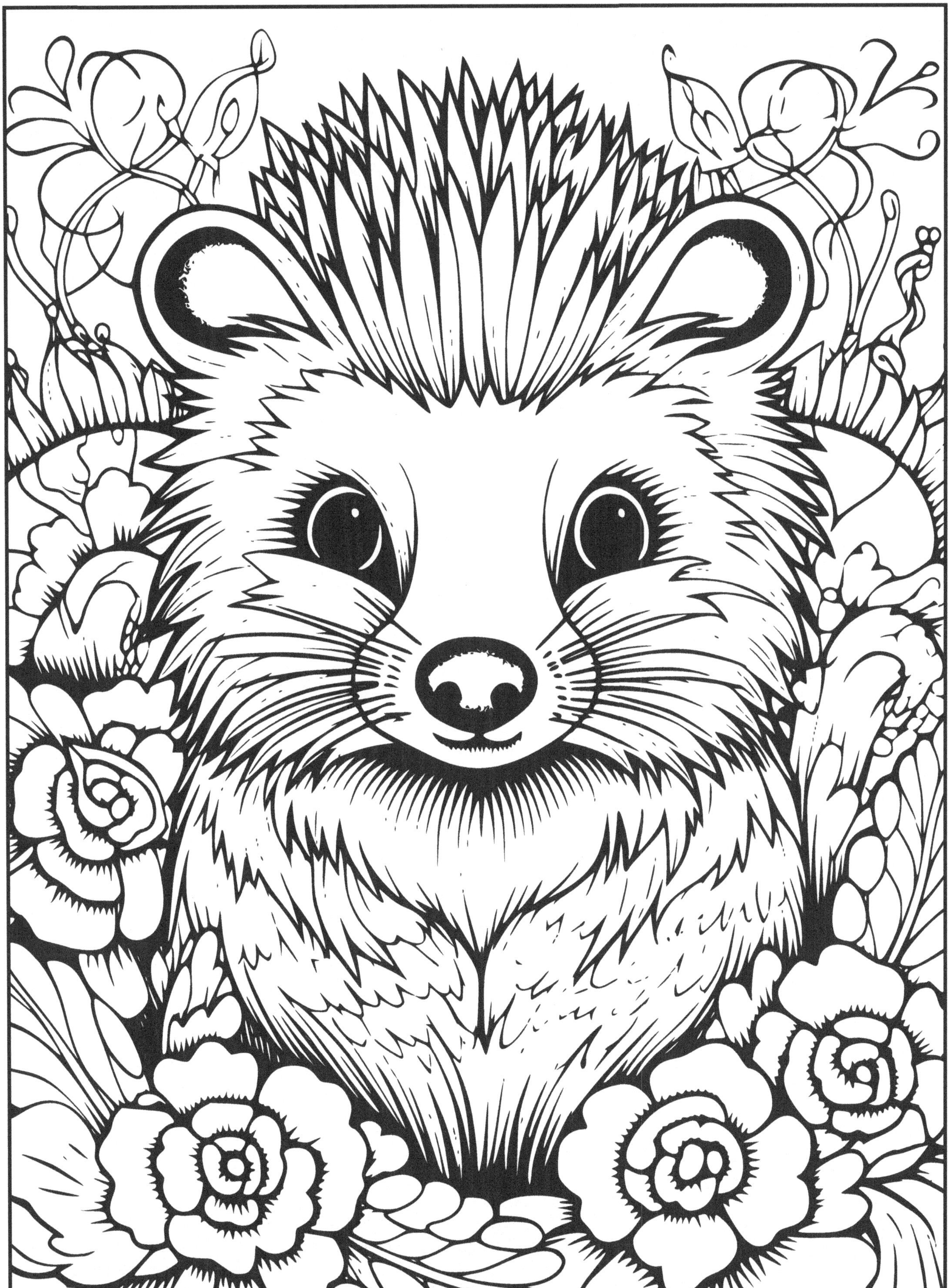

(This page intentionally left blank)

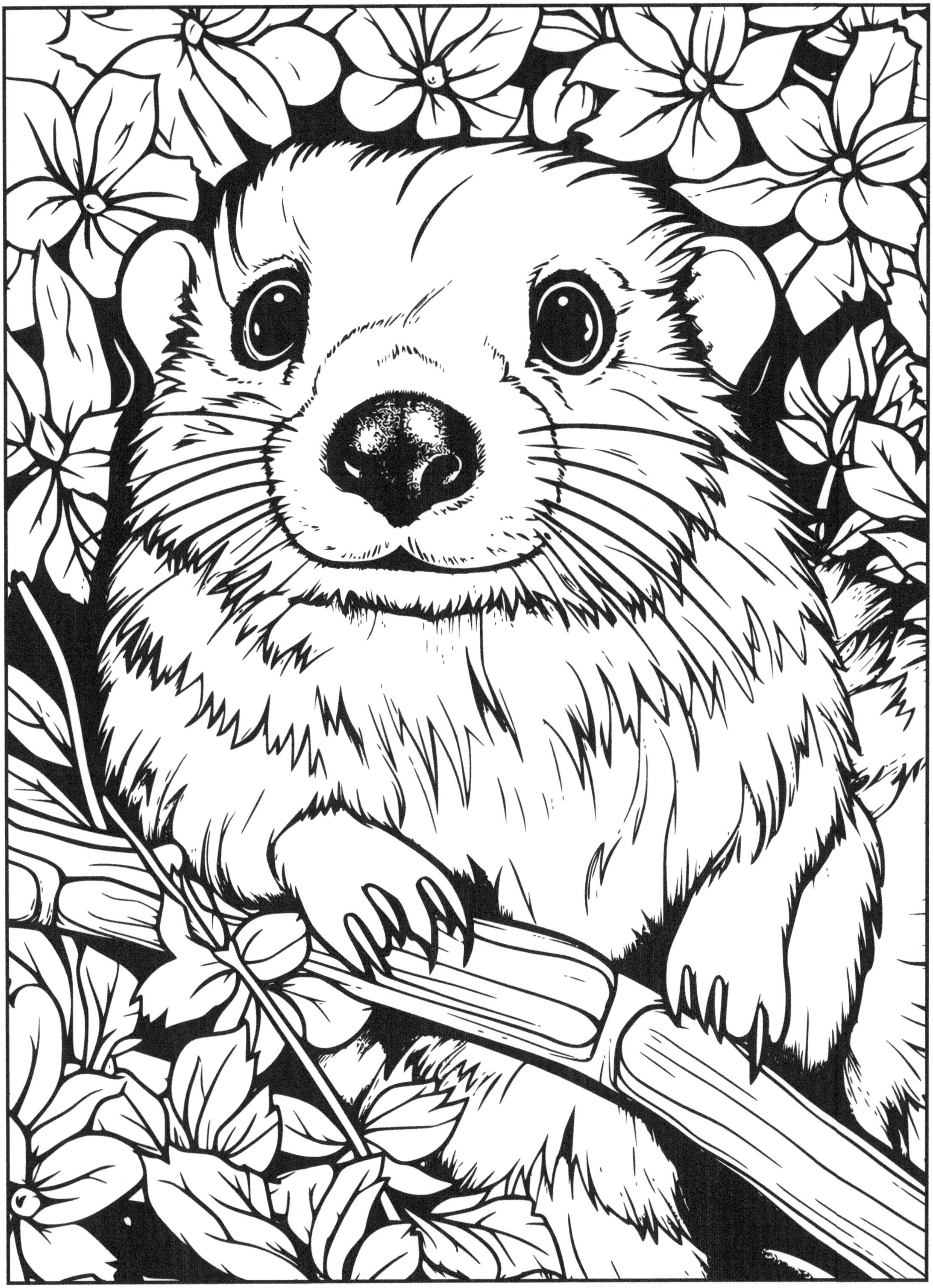

(This page intentionally left blank)

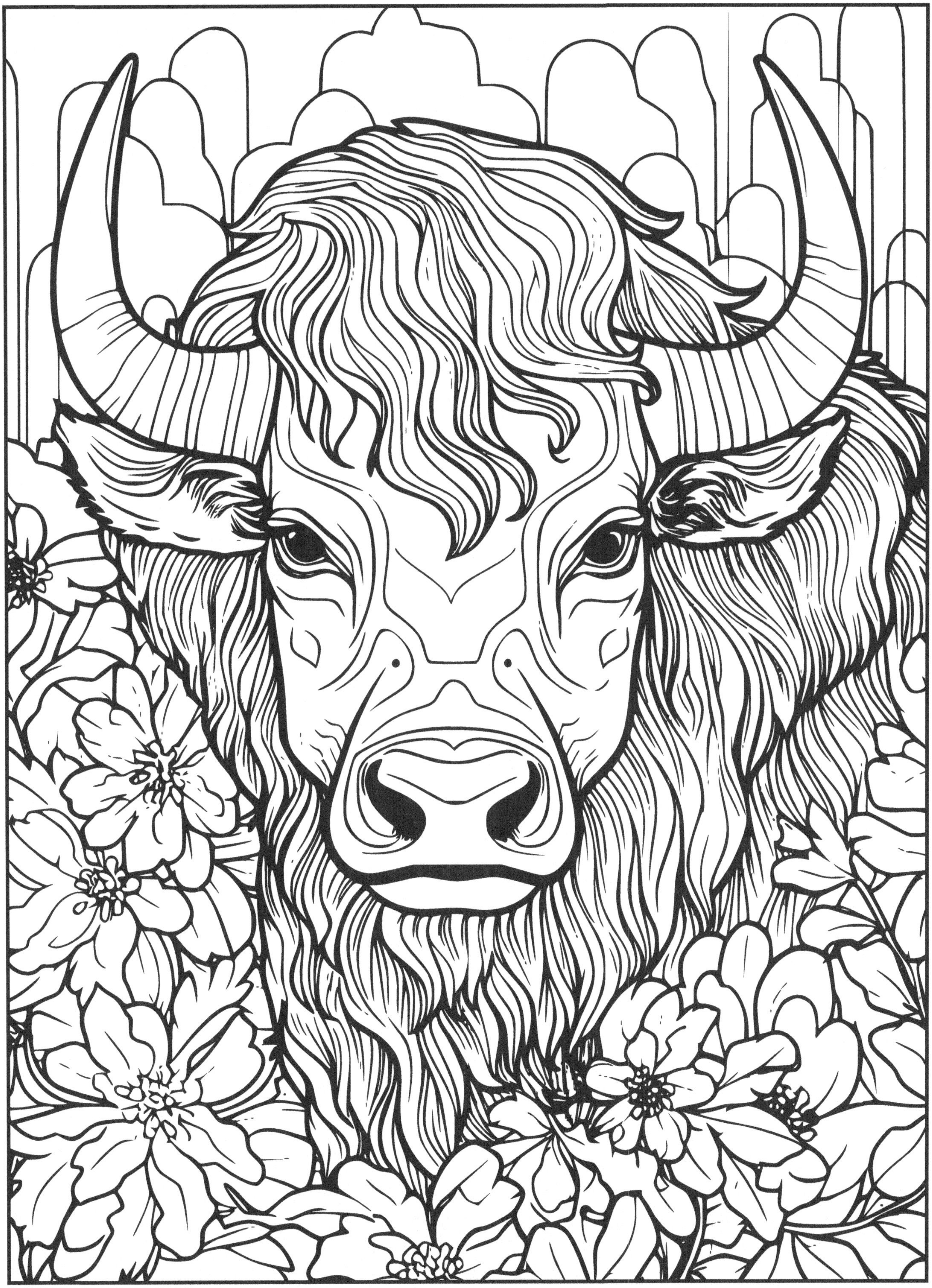

(This page intentionally left blank)

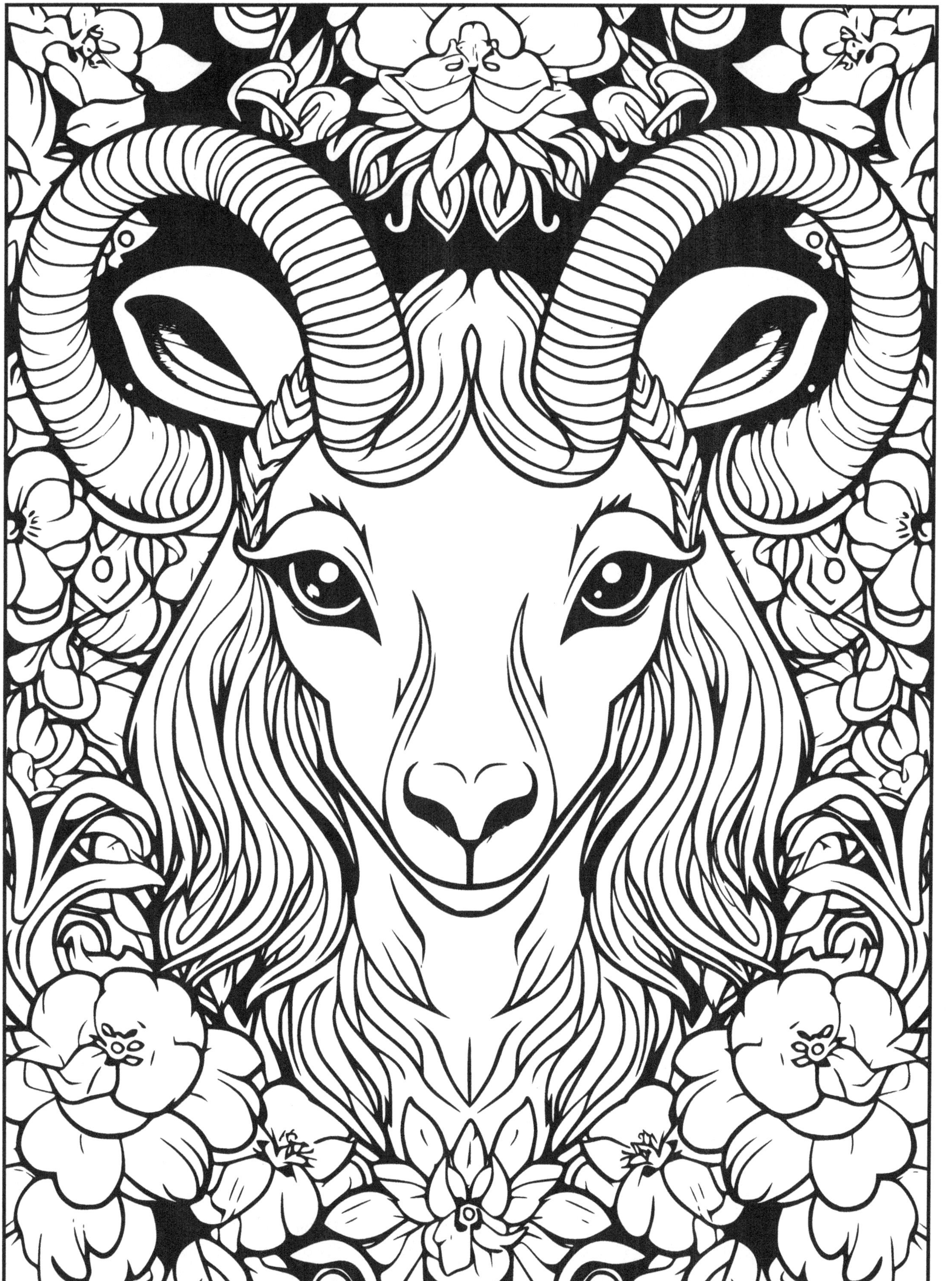

(This page intentionally left blank)

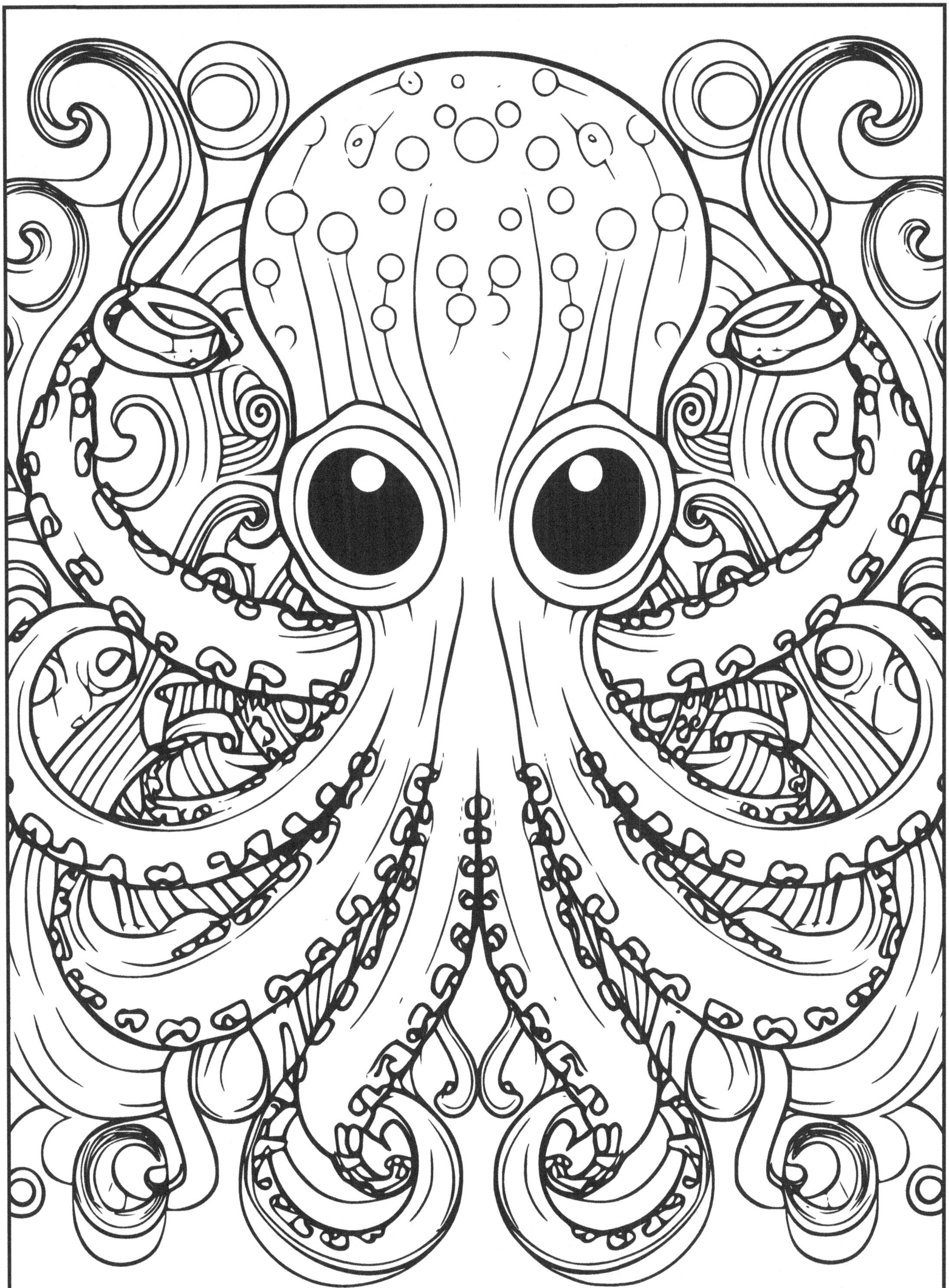

(This page intentionally left blank)

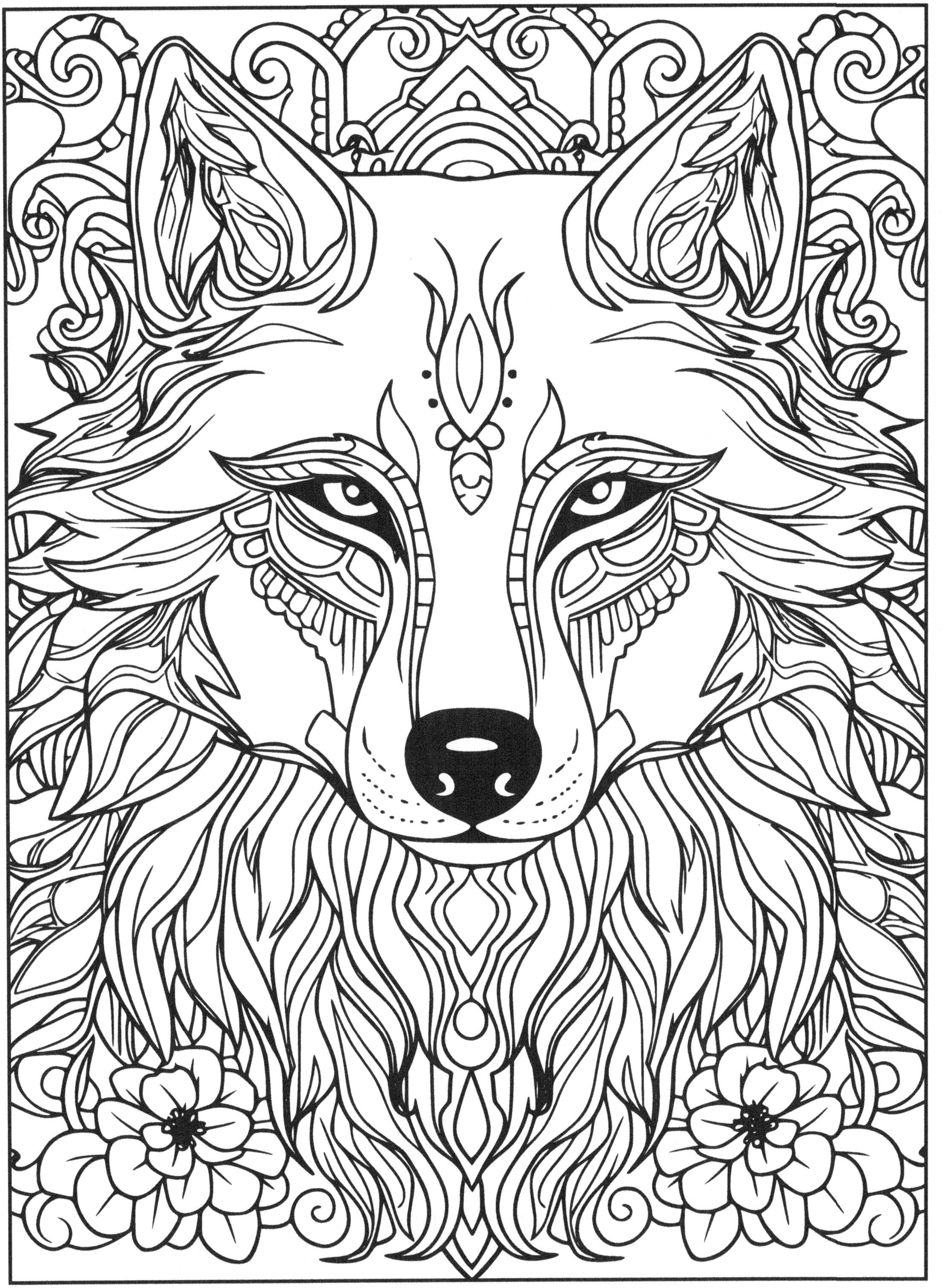

(This page intentionally left blank)

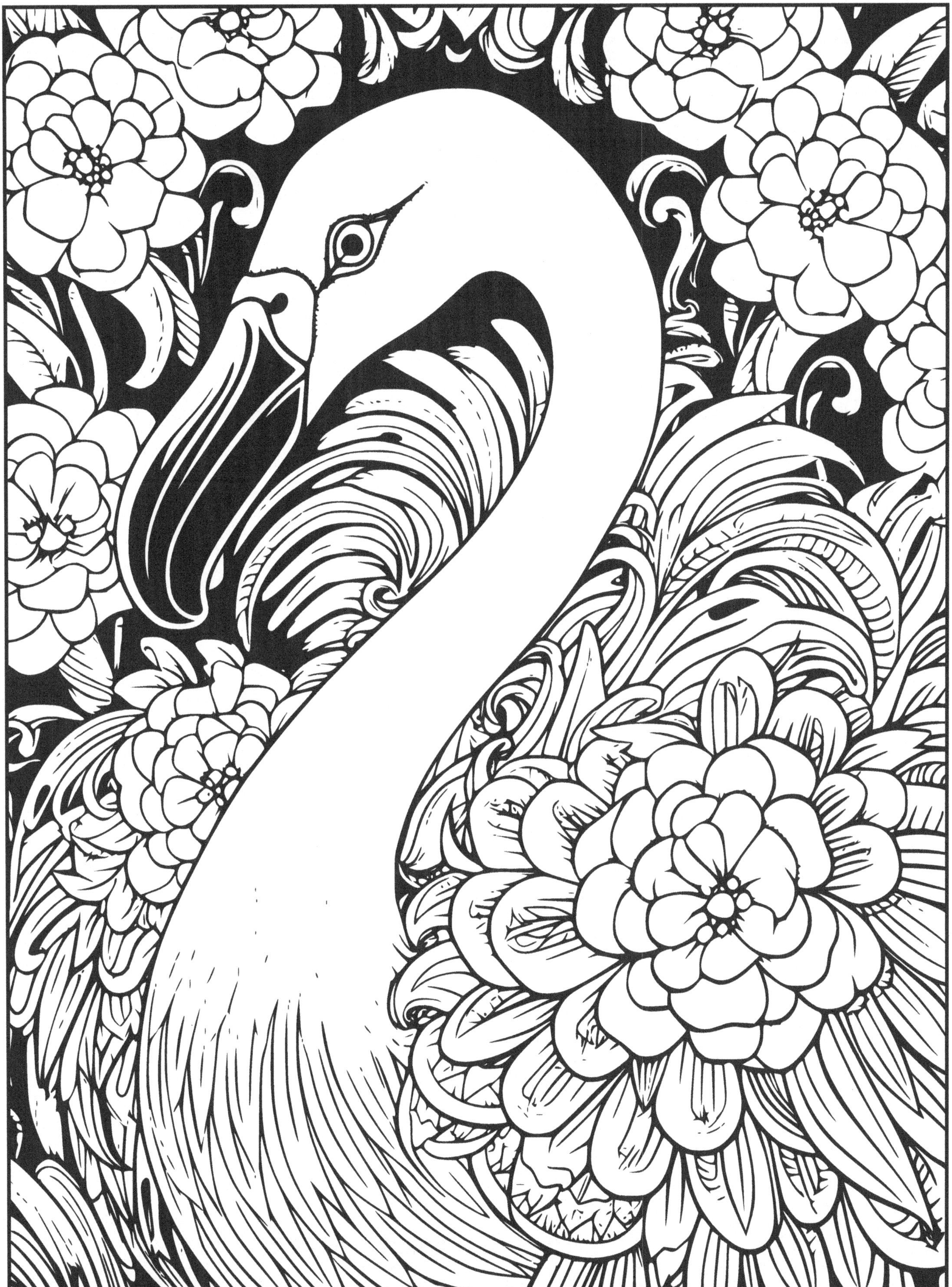

(This page intentionally left blank)

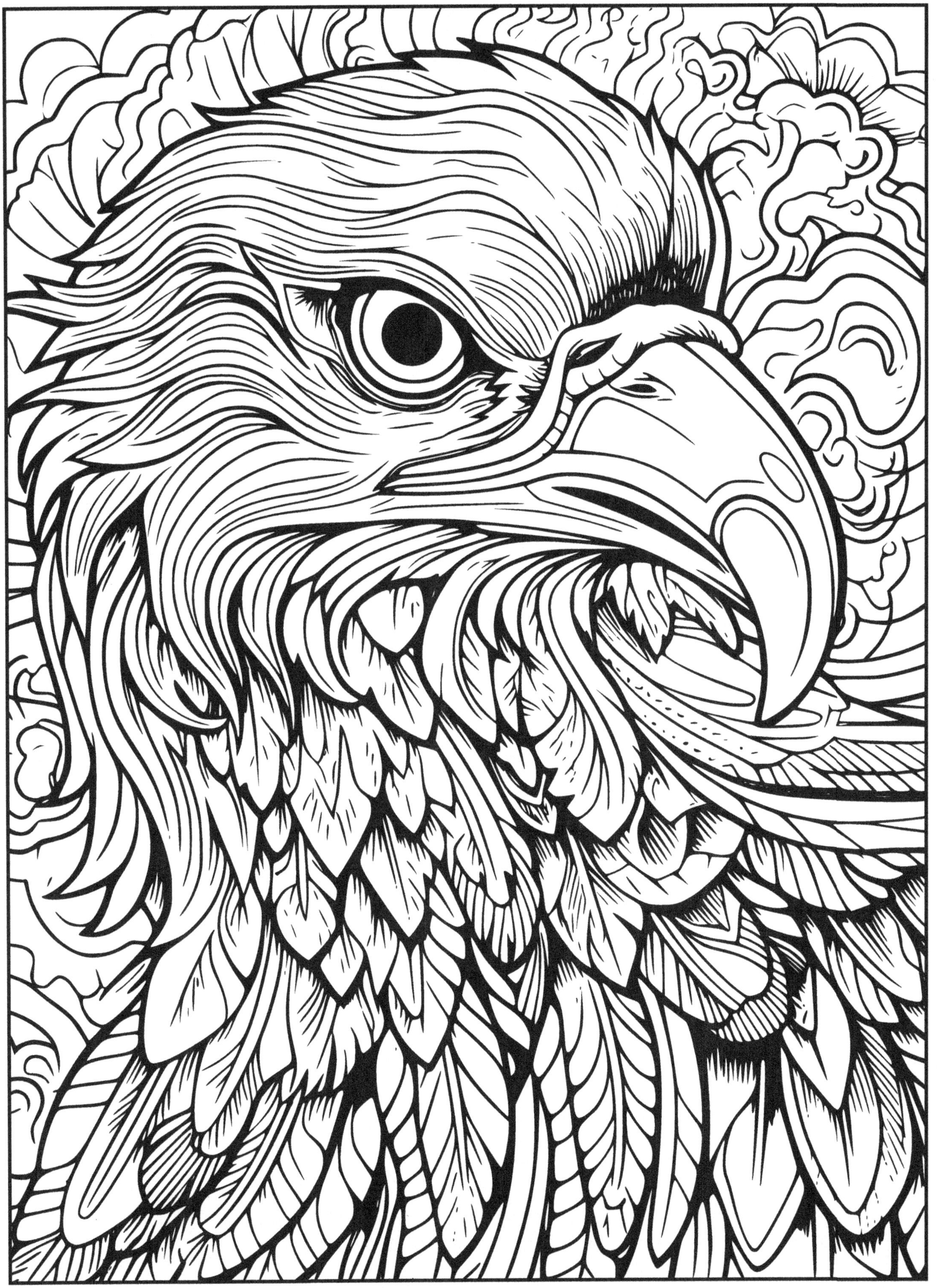

(This page intentionally left blank)

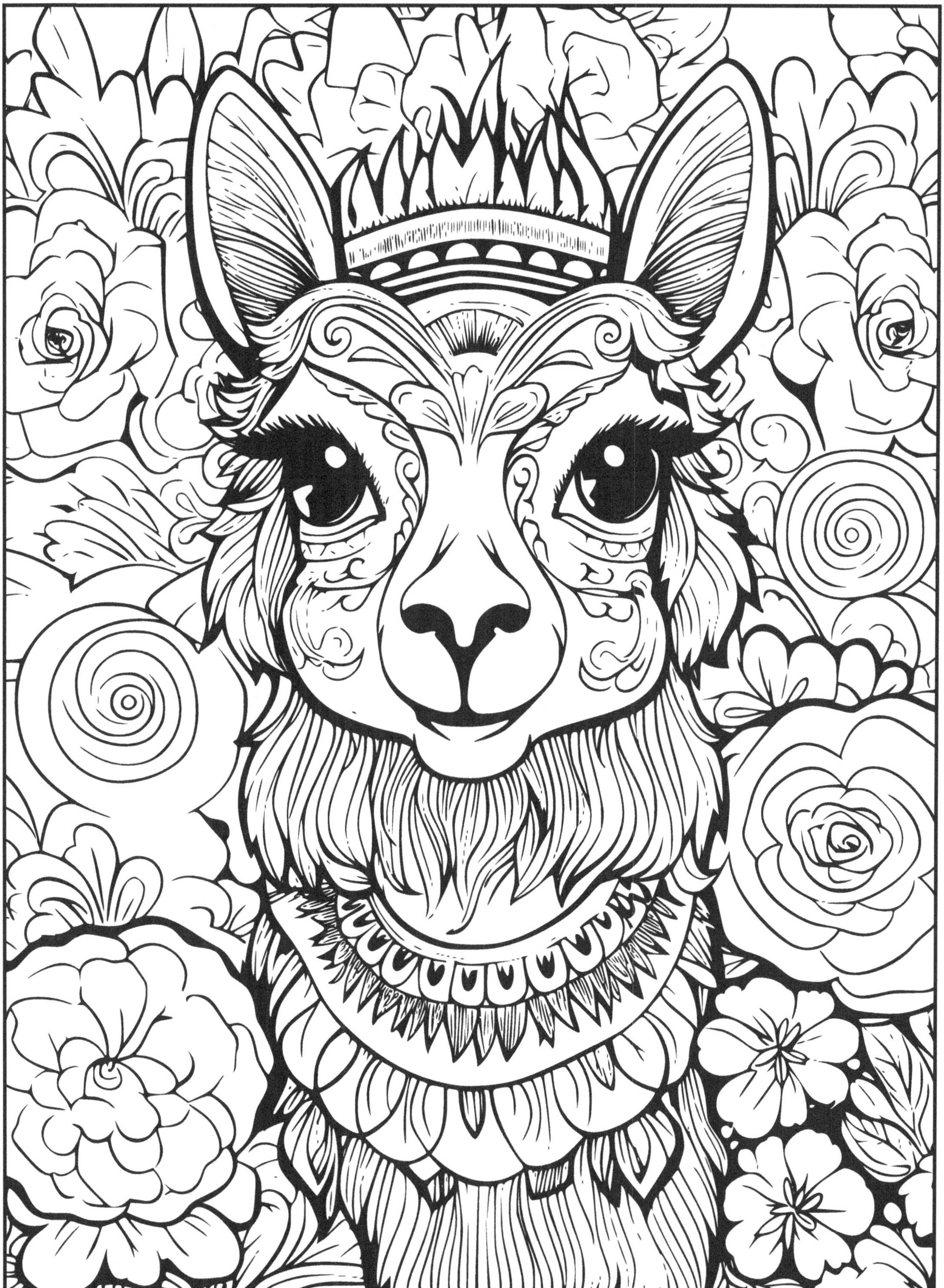

(This page intentionally left blank)

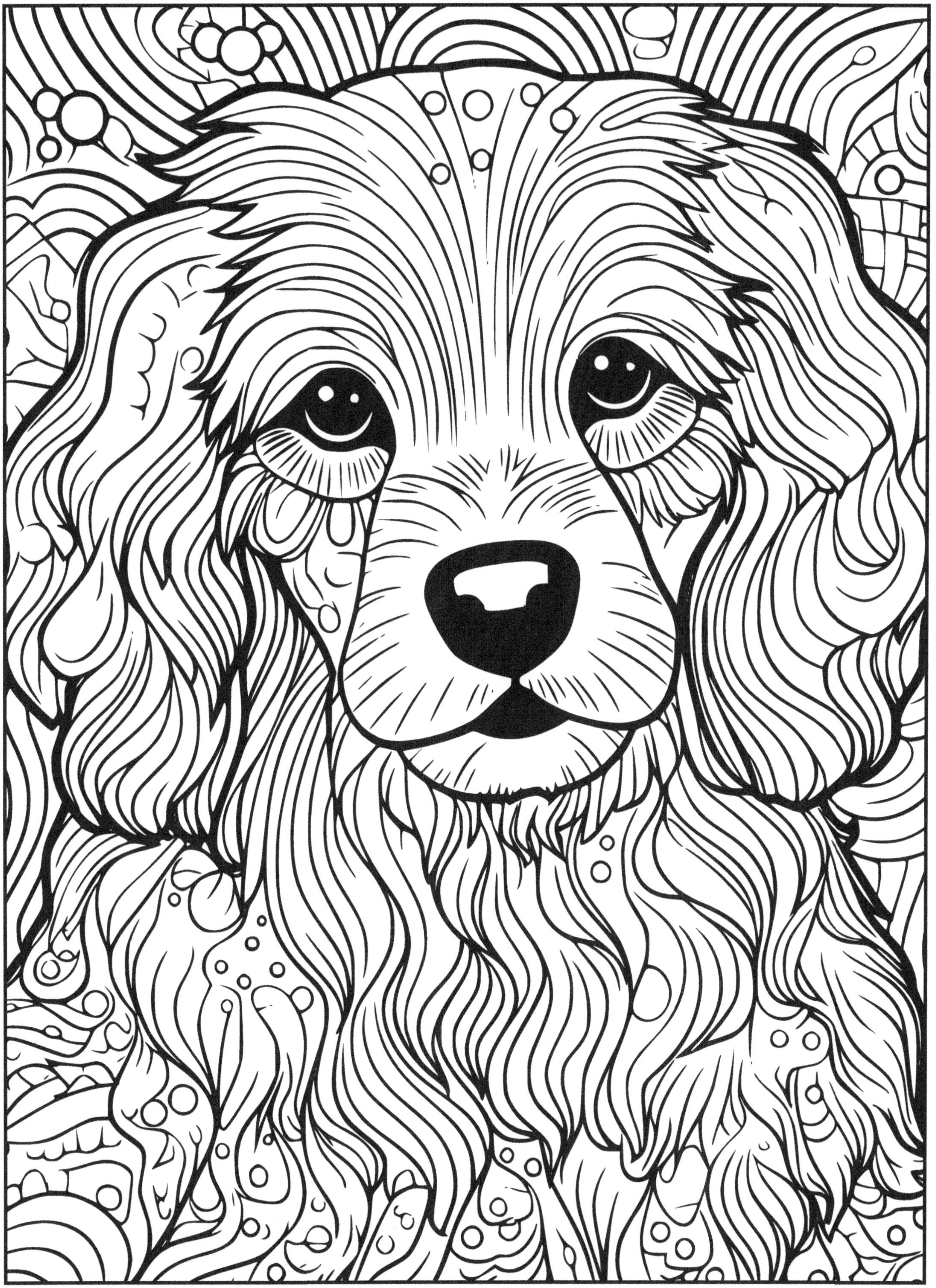

(This page intentionally left blank)

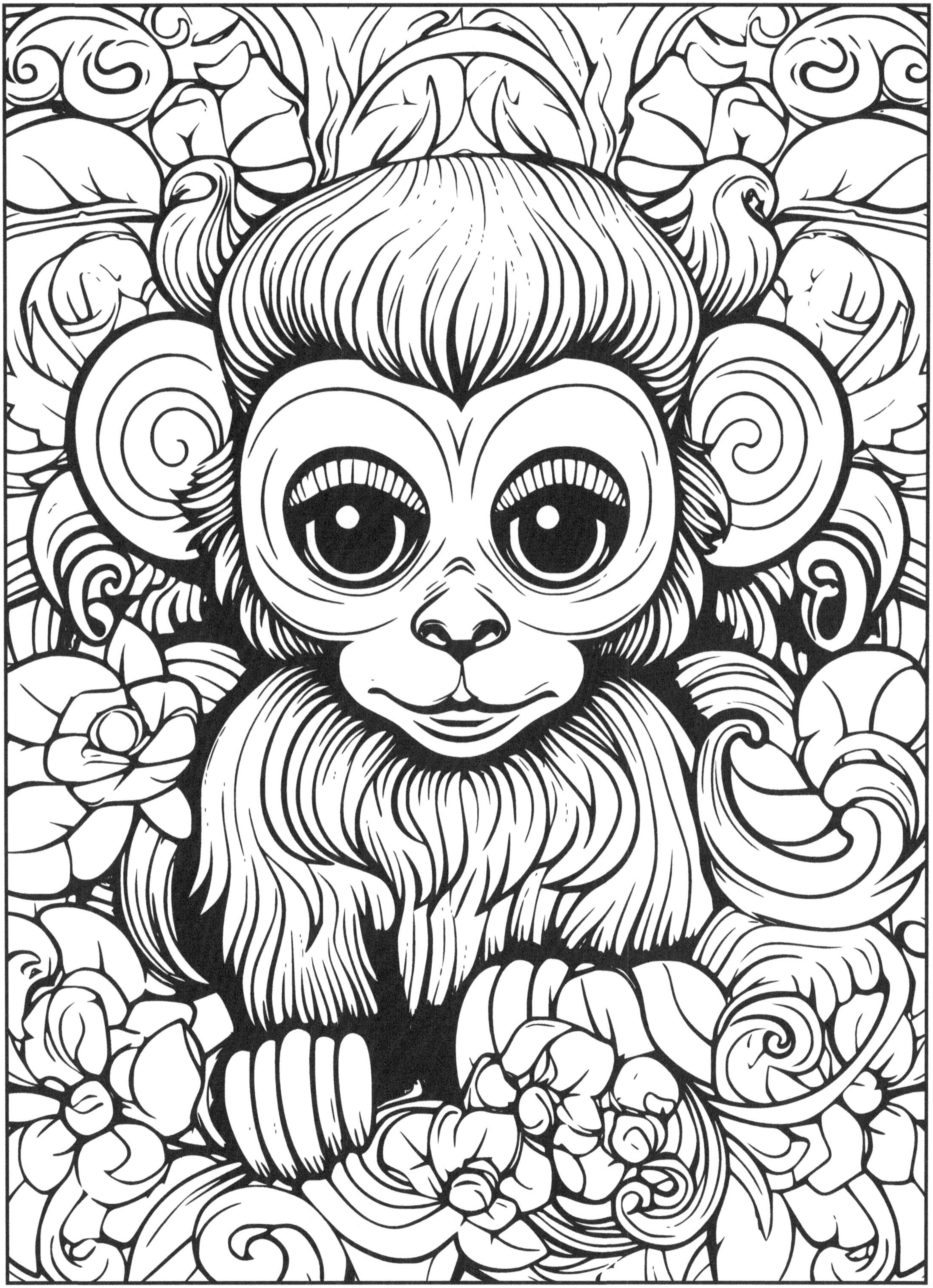

(This page intentionally left blank)

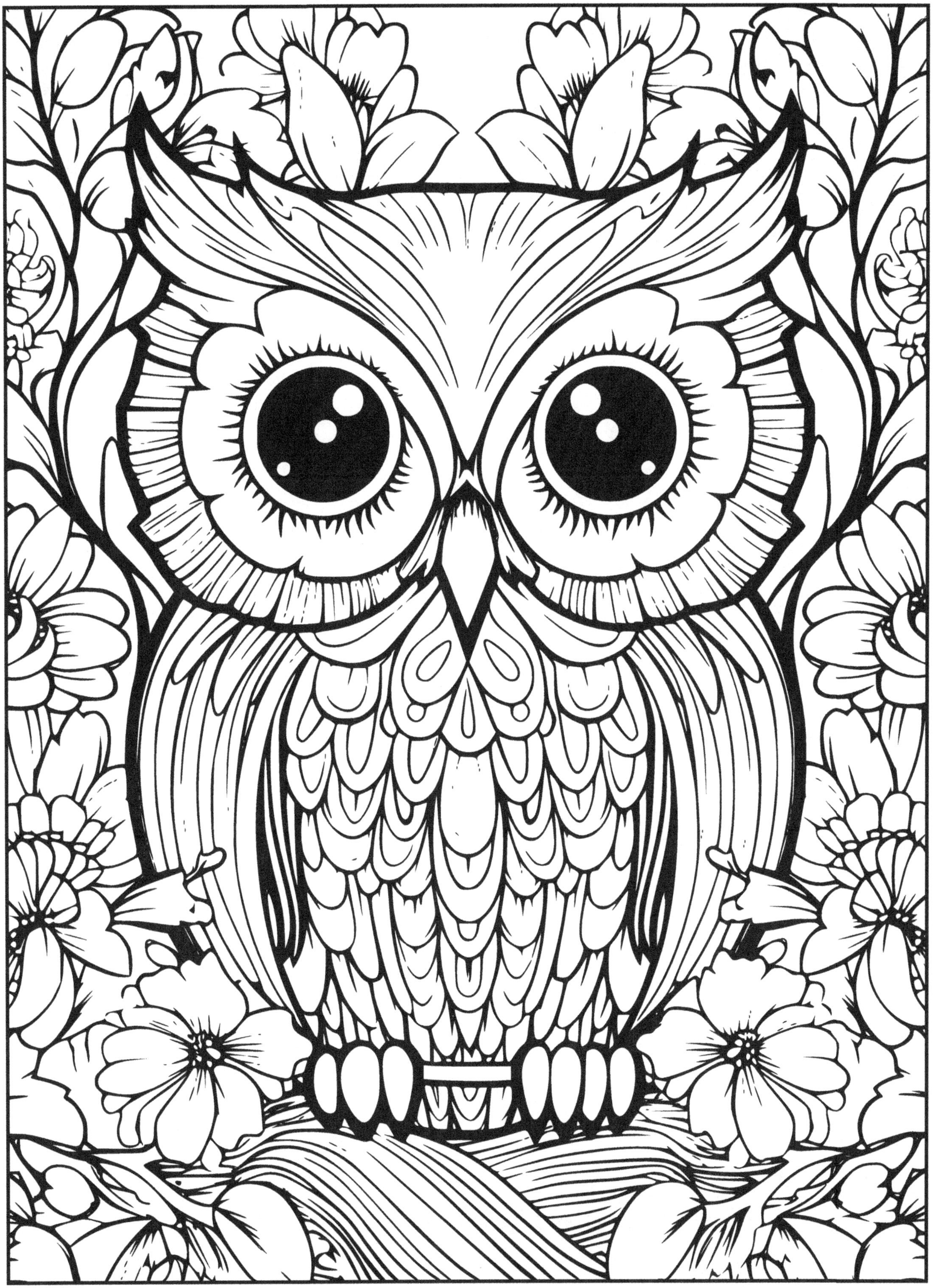

(This page intentionally left blank)

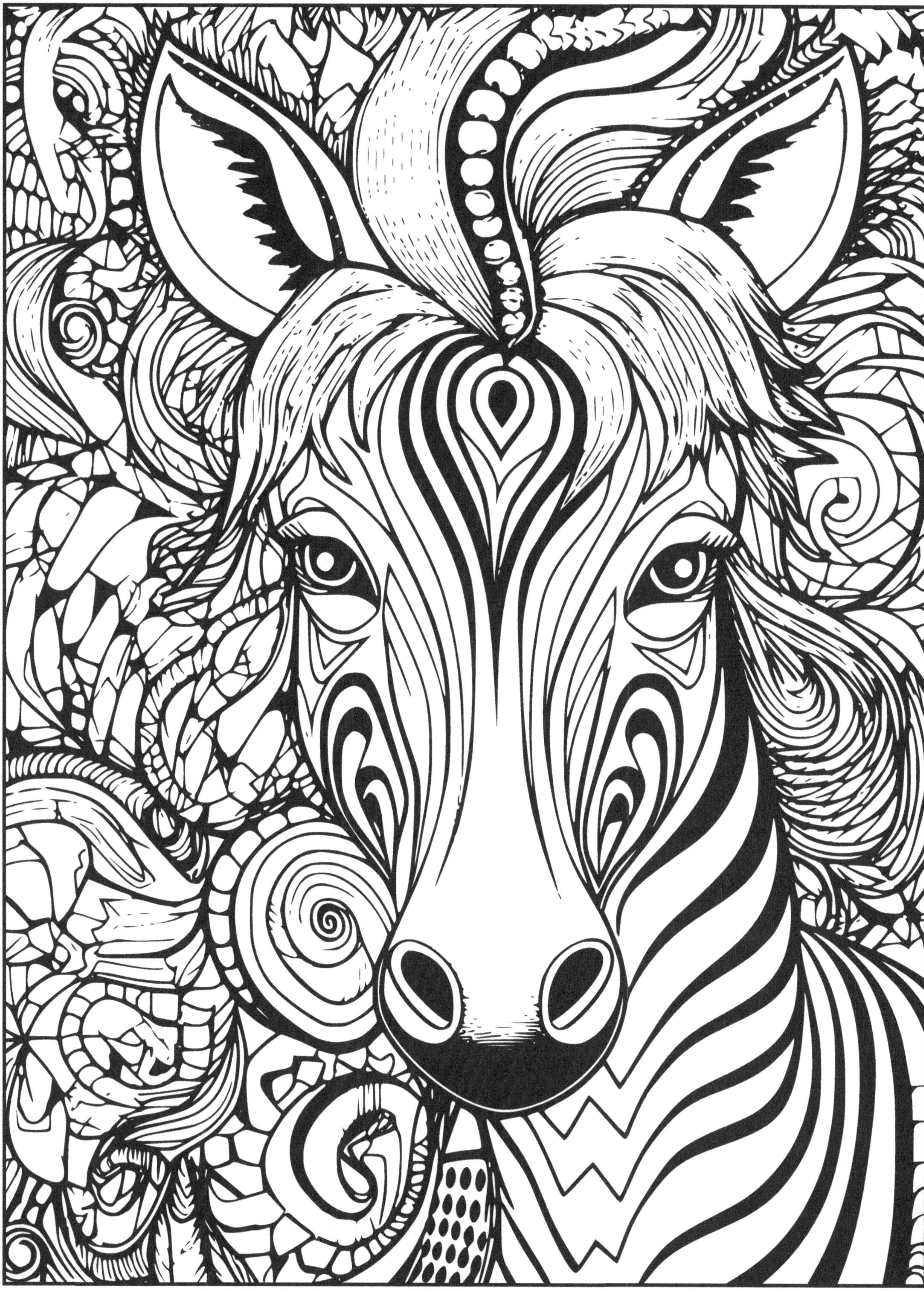

(This page intentionally left blank)

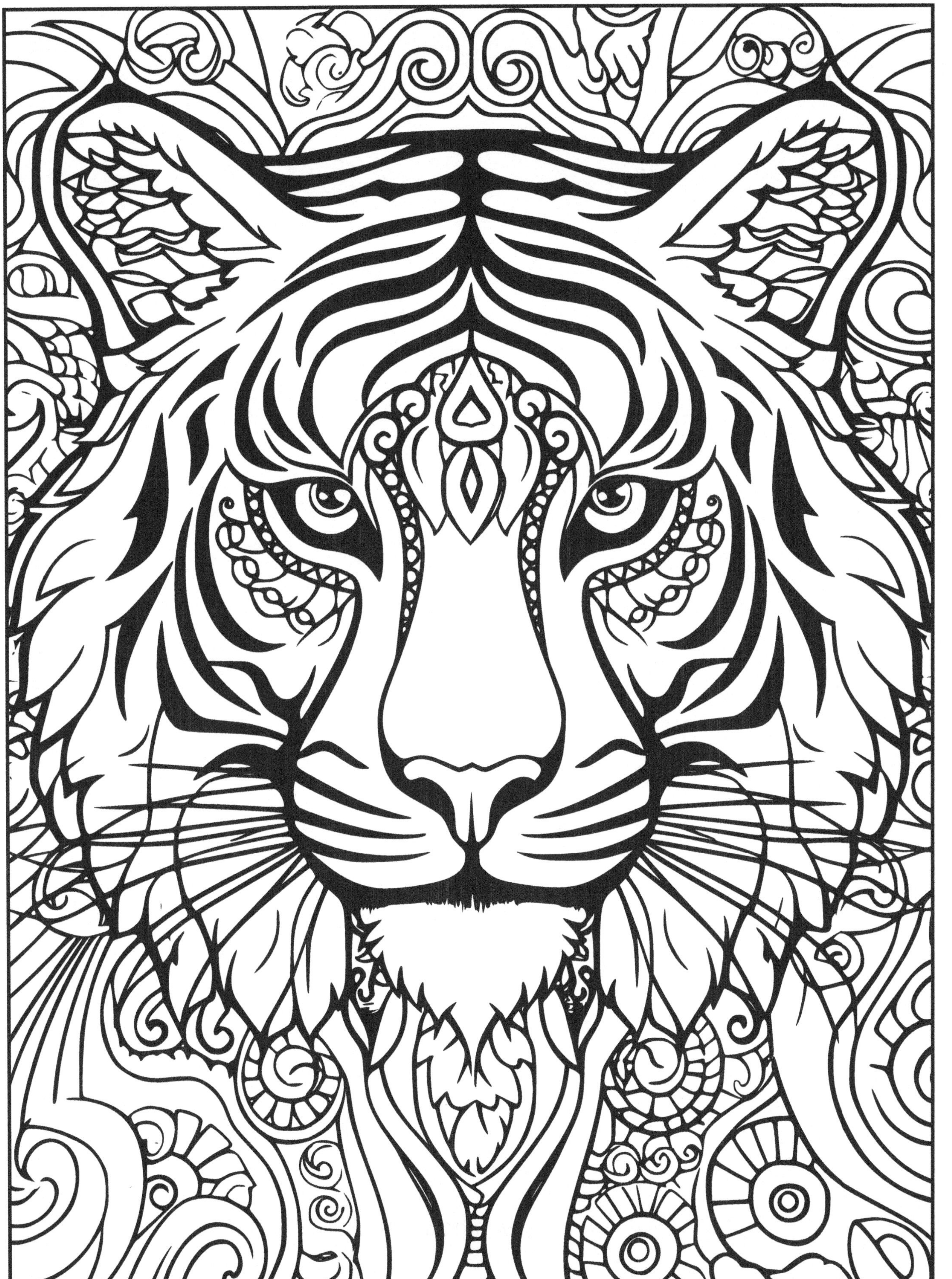

(This page intentionally left blank)

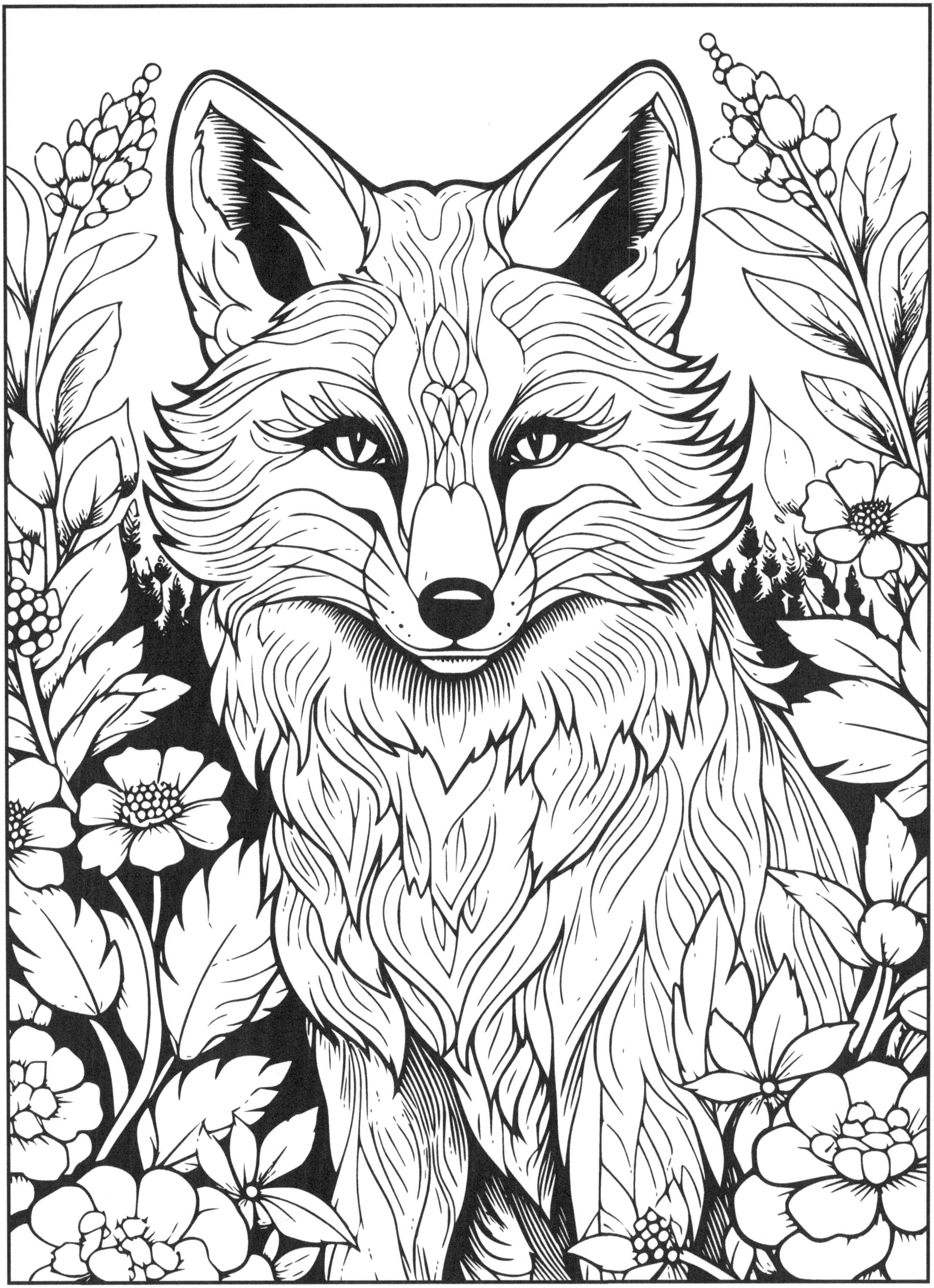

(This page intentionally left blank)

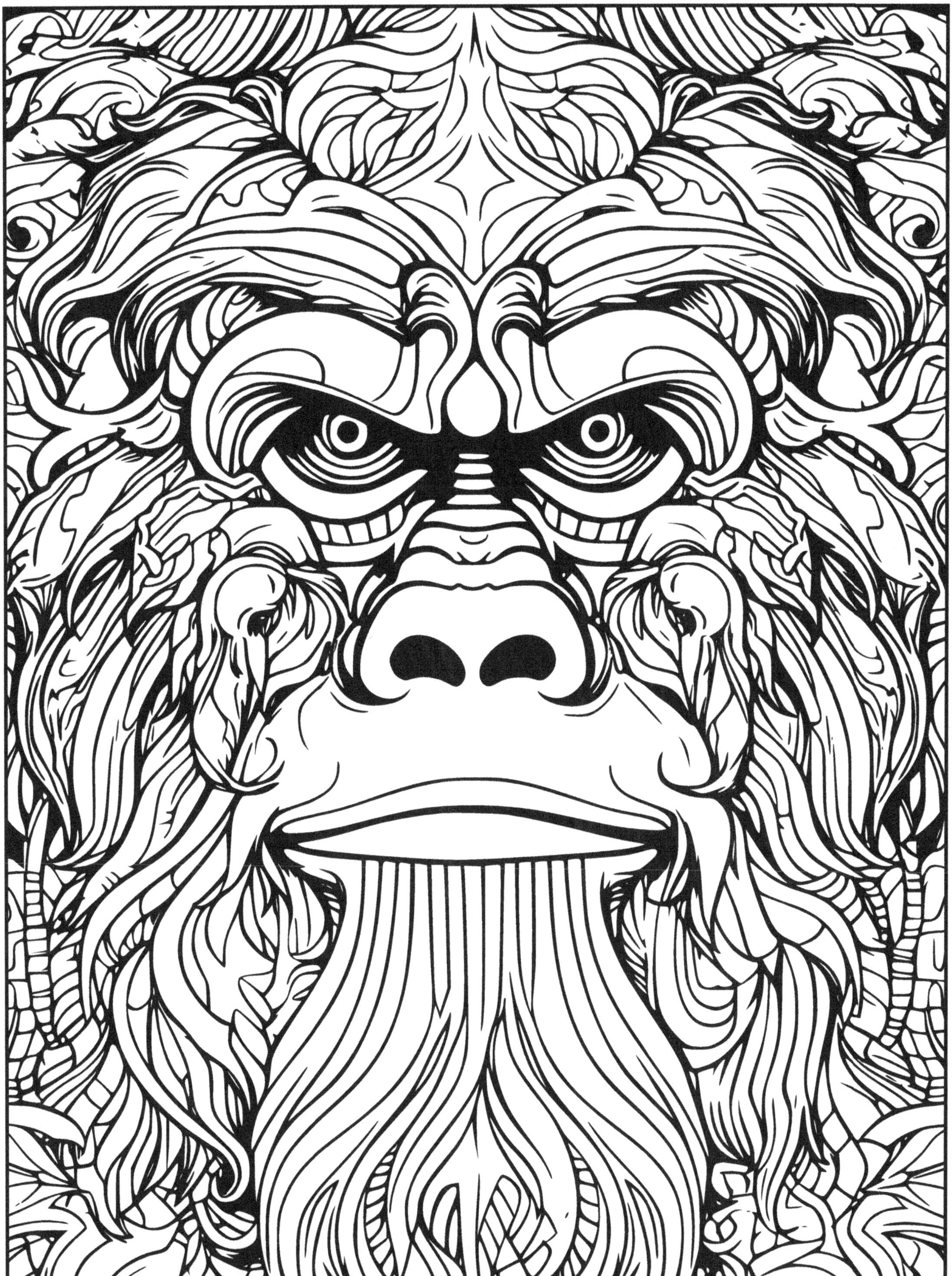

(This page intentionally left blank)

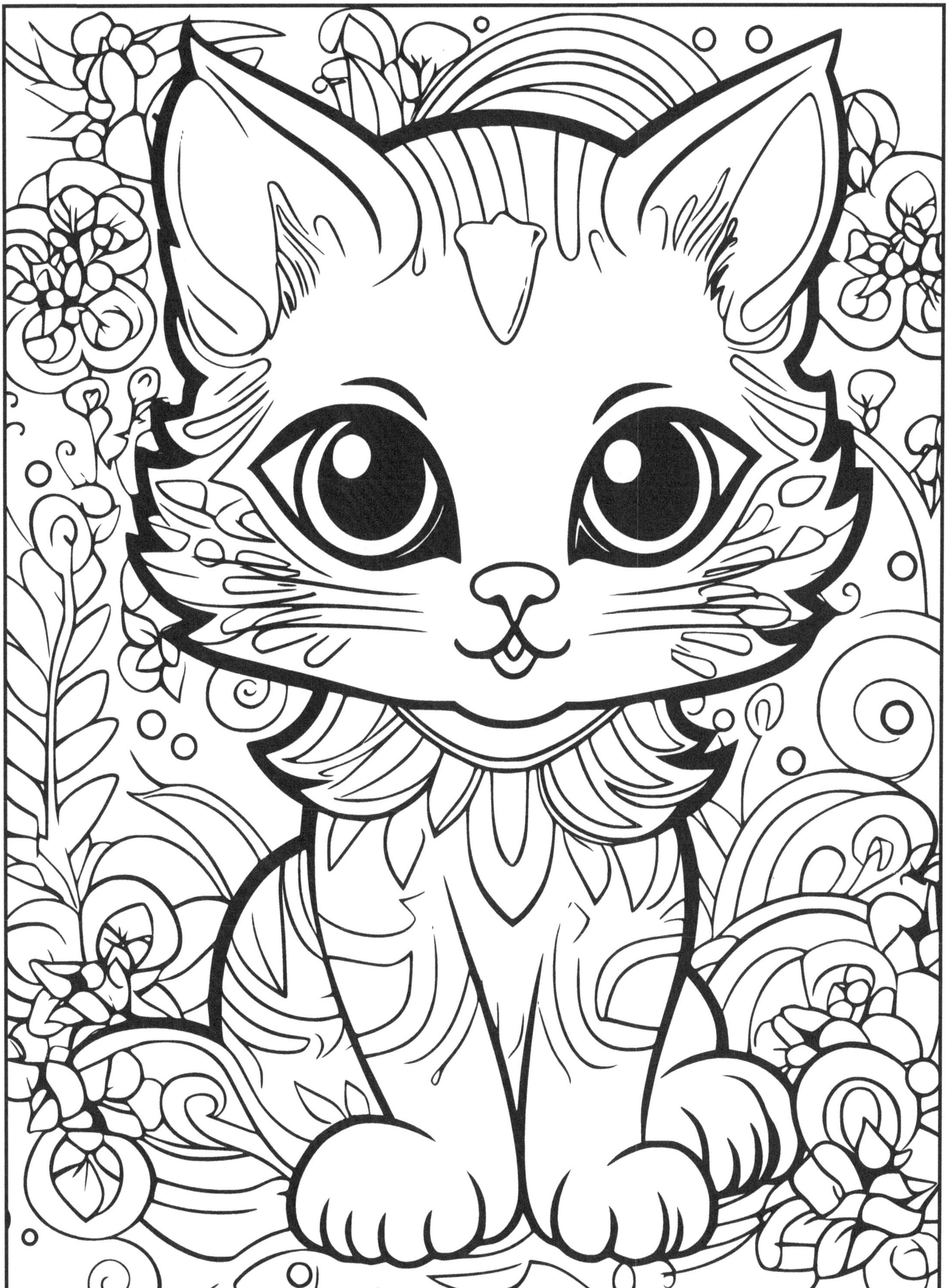

(This page intentionally left blank)

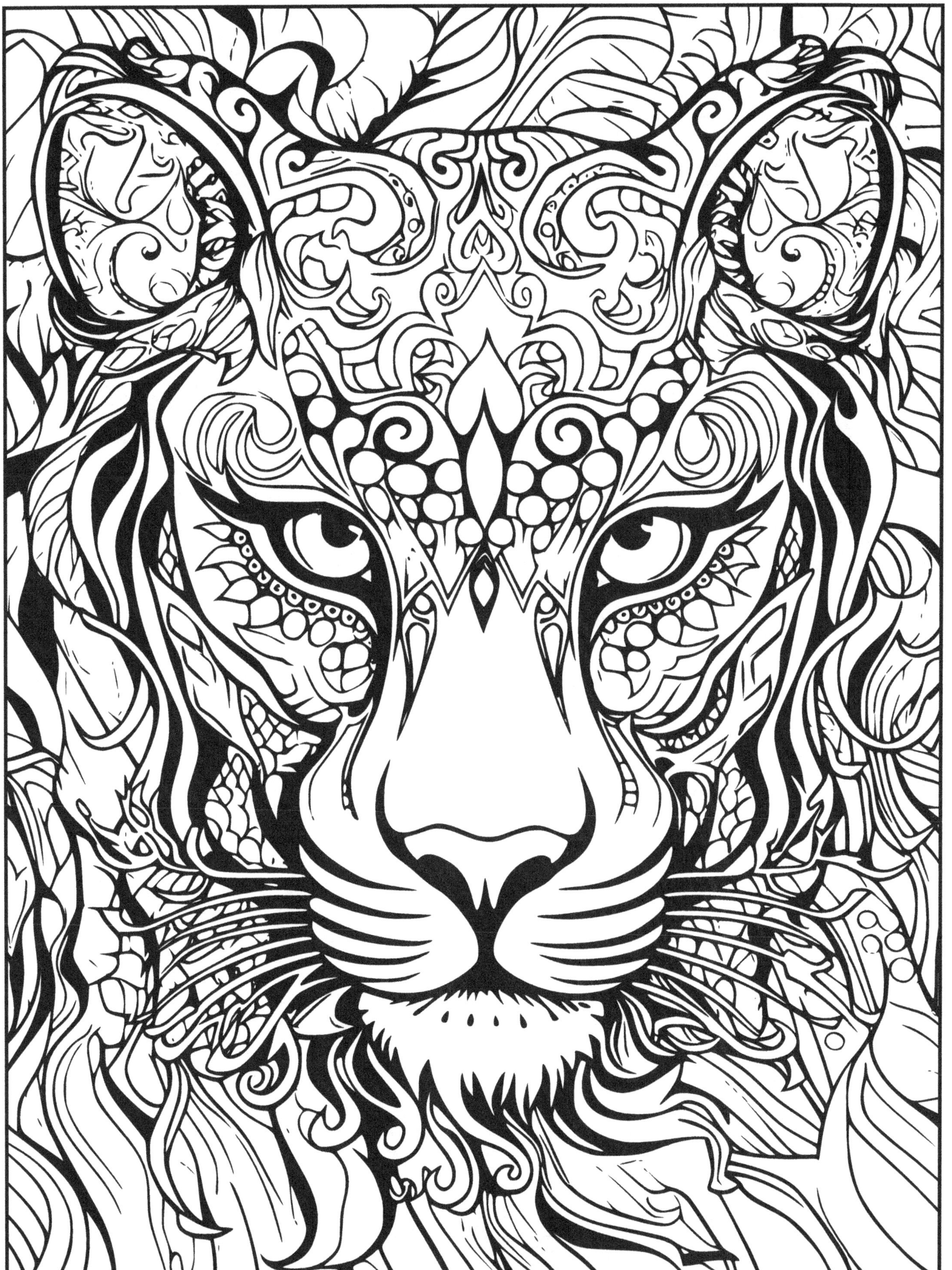

(This page intentionally left blank)

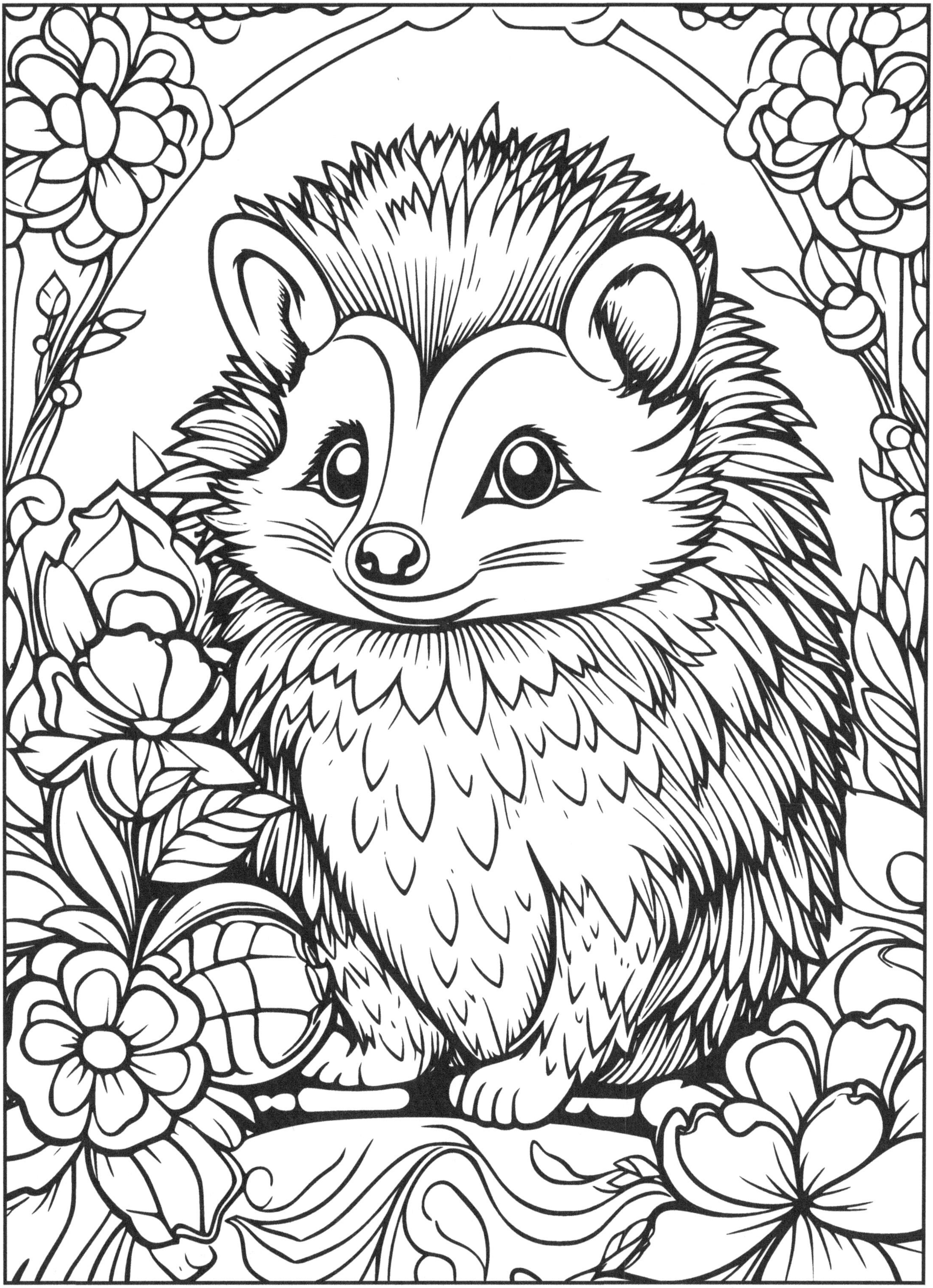

(This page intentionally left blank)

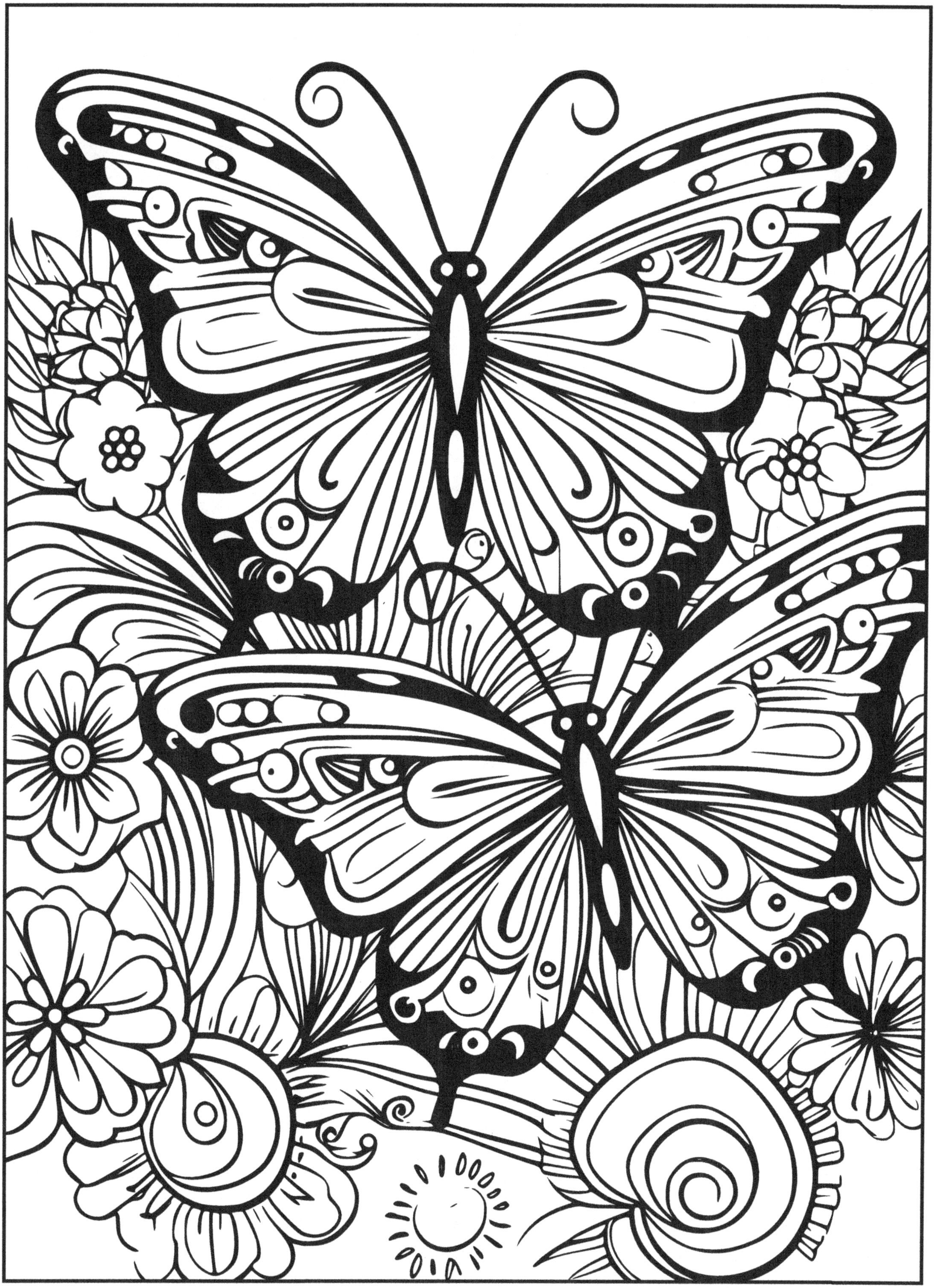

(This page intentionally left blank)

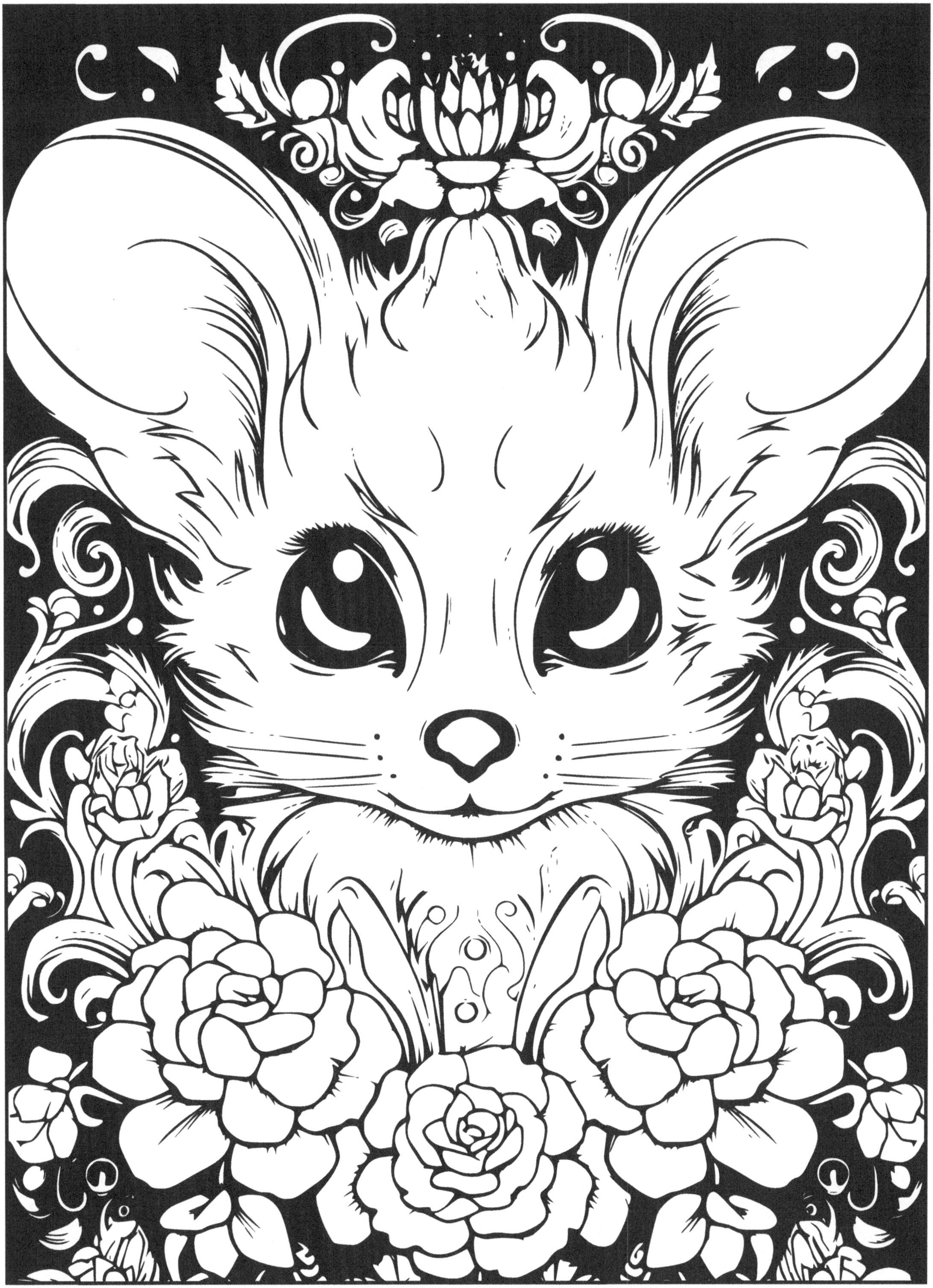

(This page intentionally left blank)

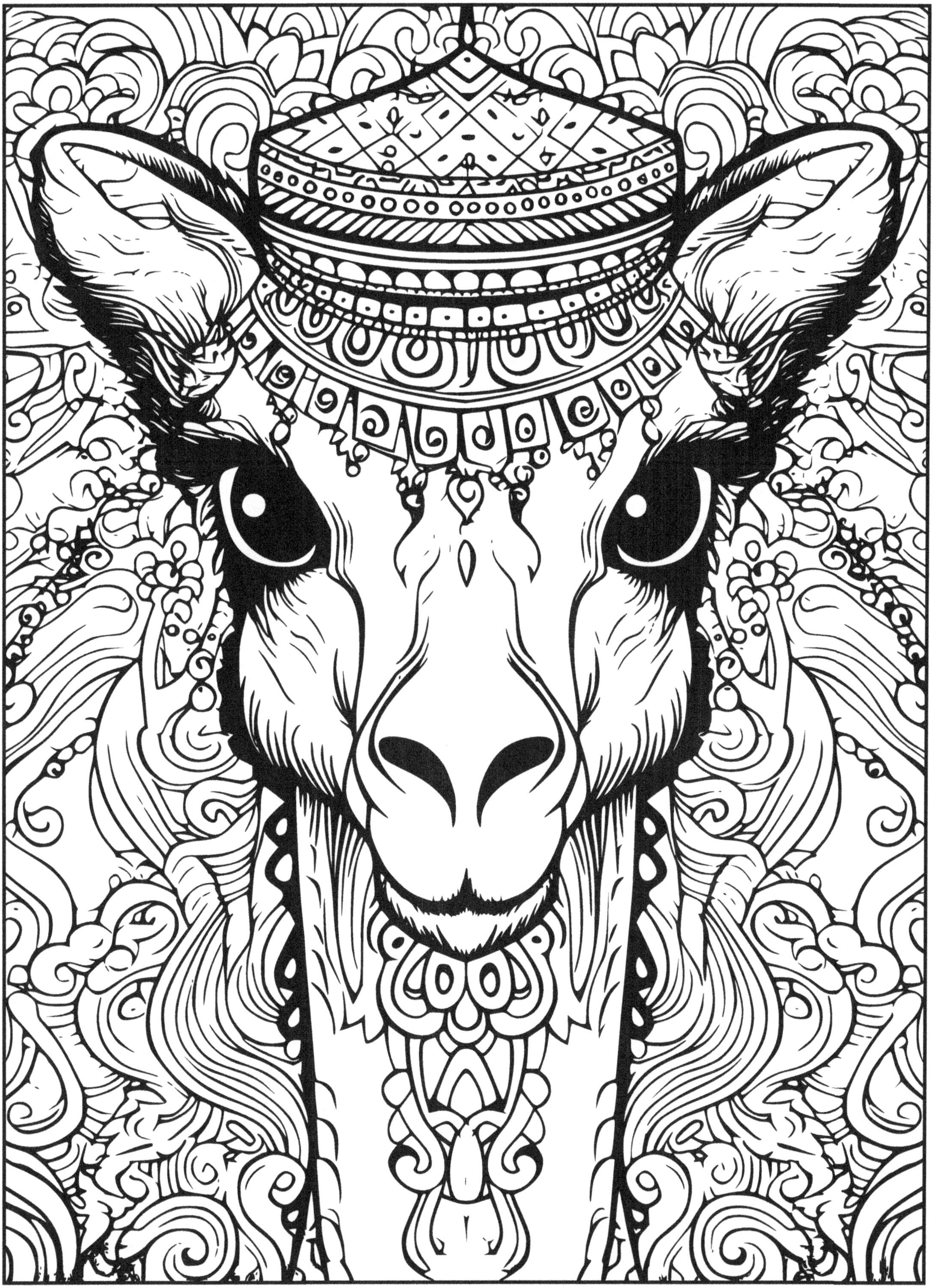

(This page intentionally left blank)

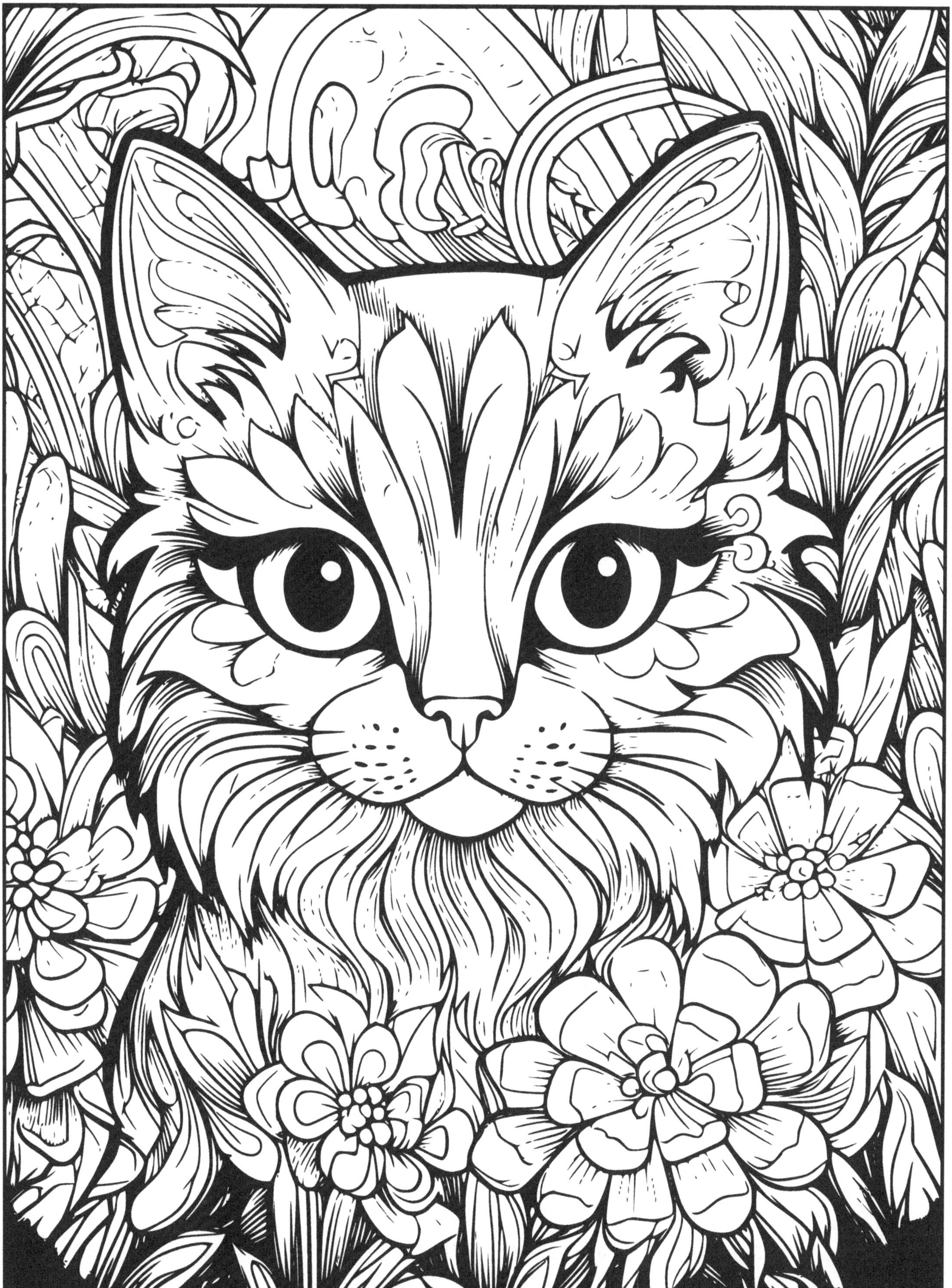

(This page intentionally left blank)

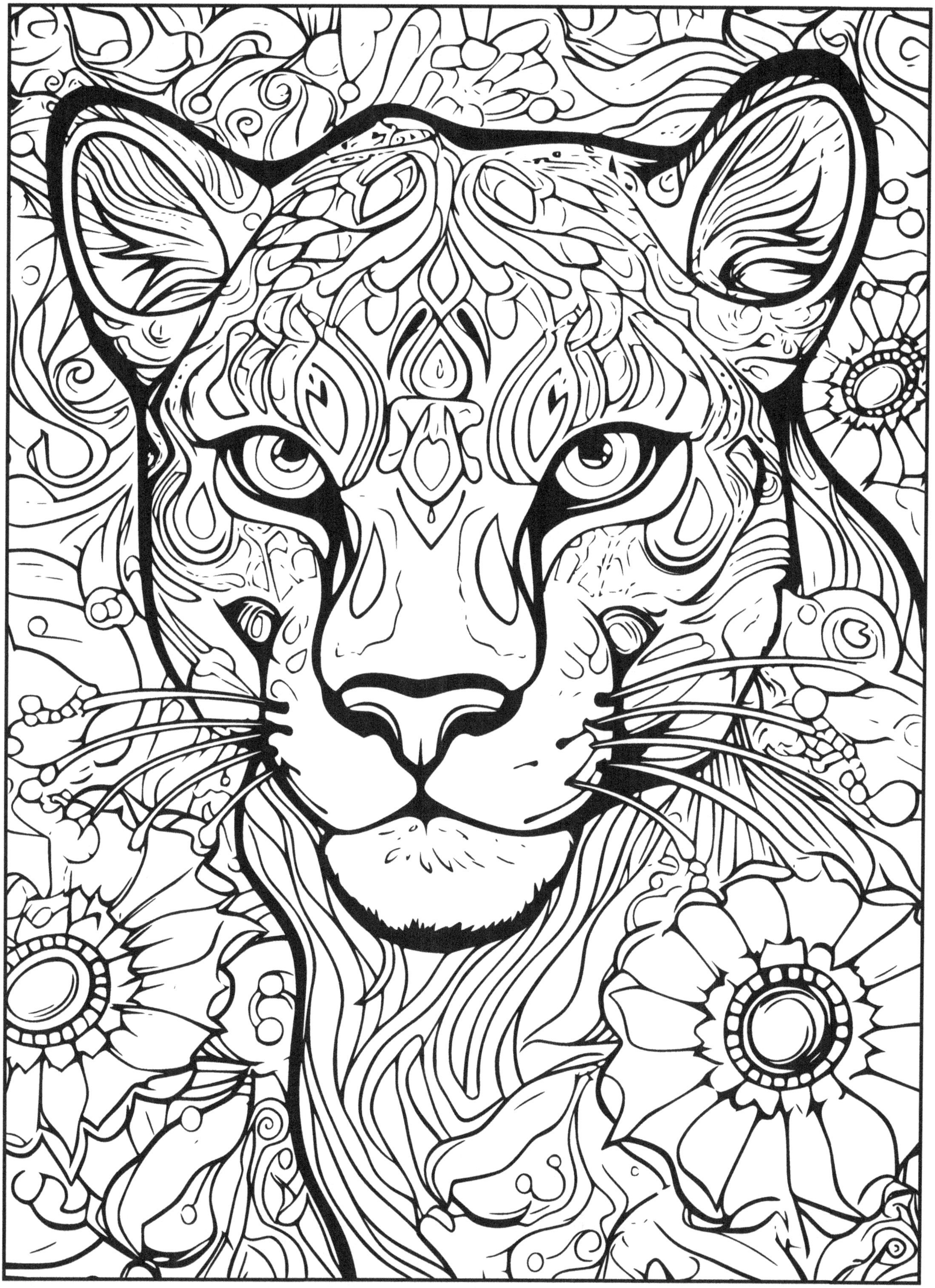

(This page intentionally left blank)

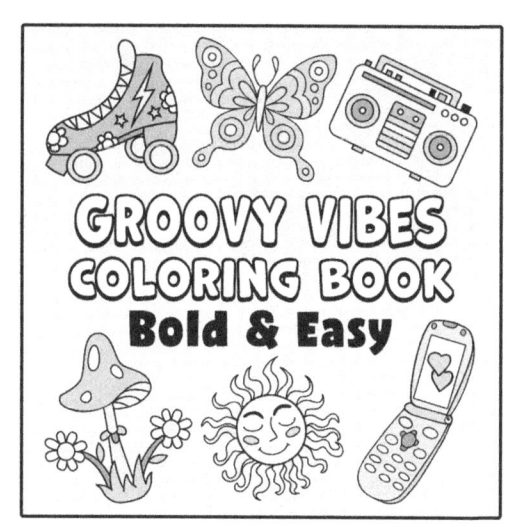

CHECK US OUT!

SAVE 20% OFF YOUR NEXT PURCHASE ON OUR WEBSITE WITH THIS CODE:

THANKYOU20

WWW.GOLDENAGEPRESS.COM

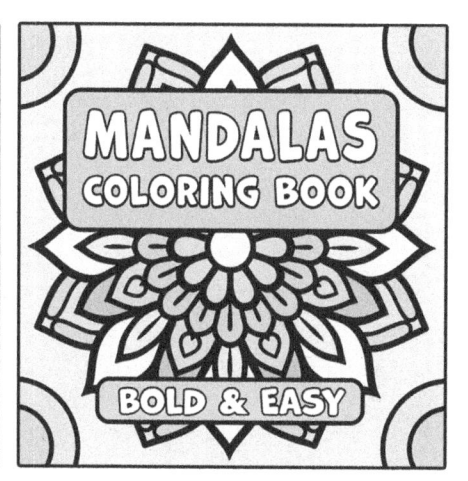

Made in the USA
Monee, IL
19 August 2025